£ 3.95

Praye

Graham Smith

PRAYER WORDS

An Exercise in Meditative Prayer

BURNS & OATES   DAVID LOVELL
PUBLISHING

First published in Great Britain 1991
Burns & Oates Ltd,
Wellwood, North Farm Road,
Tunbridge Wells, Kent TN2 3DR

First published in Australia by
David Lovell Publishing
Brunswick, Victoria 3056

ISBN (UK) 0 86012 185 2
ISBN (AUST.) 1 86355 016 X

Calligraphy by Kathi Drolet

Composition by Genesis Typesetting, Rochester, Kent
Printed and bound in Great Britain by
Biddles Ltd, Guildford and King's Lynn

Contents

Note

Unless otherwise stated, biblical quotations are from the
Common Bible (CB). Otherwise, JB = Jerusalem Bible;
NEB = New English Bible.

Bracketted references in the text in bold type are to numbered
paragraphs.

Asterisks * indicate references, which can be found organized
by paragraph number on pp. 78–80.

Books on Yoga should be read with great caution, and their
use in this book does not imply endorsement of all the
doctrines and practices recommended in them.

Preface

This is a manual for meditative prayer and there is a problem to be faced straight away. It uses the body-centres taught by Yoga as the focus of prayer and this attention to the self could invite the accusation of self-centred pietism, encouraging a private religion dedicated to the cultivation of the inner life, at the expense of commitment to the corporate life of the Church and to the secular political community. It might be argued that the spirit of it is more Hindu than Christian, seeing the "real" world as inward and spiritual, instead of sacramental, i.e. material-and-spiritual together.

I would take such views very seriously. I am aware that this book (which is based on my own daily practice) relies heavily on yogic and other disciplines and images which belong to world-views in some ways different from the Christian. For Hindus, for example, the self is certainly real enough, since it shares in the reality of God; but at the deep, spiritual level (as distinct from ordinary social life) it seems to be isolated from other souls. For Buddhists, on the other hand, the self has no real existence at all, but is a series of events like the succession of frames in a film. It is difficult to reconcile ideas like these with Christian beliefs.

Beginning with the last point, I would like to say three things in reply. First, I not only admit but gladly acknowledge that I am deeply indebted to Yoga and other non-Christian systems and methods, and gratefully use their experience, truth and wisdom. At the same time, I am ready to part company with them when necessary and to say, as it were: "It has been good to

7

travel together along the Way. Thank you for your help. Now we must part, as friends. We shall meet together again within the Kingdom of God."

Secondly, the individual, praying "alone" with God, is still very much part of the "team" – the Church, the Body of Christ, the Communion of Saints – and of the human race as a whole. We take our part in team work-outs and in playing the game itself; but we need to do individual training as well. Without our own "private" prayer-exercises, we cannot play our full part in the team game. This is especially true in the modern world, where people are under stress and pressures of various kinds, factors which are likely to increase rather than diminish. We have to be "fit" to meet the demands of life, with a quiet mind and a hopeful spirit, as we take our place alongside our sisters and brothers in the dangerous and wonderful enterprise to which God calls us. (See also **5**, **6** and **187**.)

Finally, I would remind you that our Lord himself made time and space to be "alone" with God, often in desert places. He needed that element in his life and so surely do we. We have, as yet, only hints and glimpses of what took place during those hours of prayer and communion with the Father. Surely part of it was taken up with praying for his disciples, for the multitudes who came to him for help, for his enemies, and for the multifarious needs of creation; but I would suppose that part of it was devoted to simply being with the Father and entering more deeply into that sublime fellowship. It may be that Jesus at times reflected on Psalm 139:13: "I will give thanks unto thee, for I am fearfully and wonderfully made: marvellous are thy works, and that my soul knoweth right well." In any case, it is certainly right for us so to do.

ruah

Introduction

1. This is not a book of prayers or a book about prayer. It is a prayer-book, a sustained exercise in meditative prayer.

ᕔ

2. When I began to compose this book, I had in mind Christian readers, but with a vague thought at the back of my mind that it might be usable by some Hindus. As I worked on the material and at the same time read some books originally produced in the sixties by radical theologians like Thomas Altizer and Alistair Kee, and also some contemporary writing, I began to wonder if it might be usable by some who are, from the conventionally orthodox point of view, "atheists". Of course, they would have to make modifications of the book, but that will be the case with many users, of various sorts. The point that struck me was that the book is, in a sense, based on the human person as such, and the exercises are geared to the human body. This is because the method is yogic and Yoga is essentially human: yogis may believe in God or not, although I suppose most of them do. So the method might be usable as a humanist or simply human exercise. It is not for me, a Christian, to say! The atheist or humanist or Buddhist must judge. But if it proved to be the case, I would be more than pleased and thankful.

ᕔ

3. Like most manuals, e.g. on how to drive a car, the instructions appear at first to be complicated, but when you have gone through them a few times, the procedure becomes quite simple.

4. In any case, you do not have to follow the *method* of prayer described if it does not suit you. You could simply use the *material* as a source for meditation and prayer; and there are Bible references for each prayer-word on pp. 109–111.

5. The book could be used by an individual or, e.g. by the conductor of a one-to-one or group retreat, or by the leader of a group assembled for worship or corporate meditation. Material can easily be selected and adapted to meet various needs. I hope that the arrangement of the book in numbered paragraphs, and the indices of book references (pp. 102–108), Bible passages (pp. 109–111), subjects, themes, biblical and holy Names (pp. 112–114) and authors, books, individuals (pp. 115–117), will be of practical help here.

6. I assume that many, perhaps most, of the people who use this book will normally be engaged in other prayer exercises in addition to this – corporate, liturgical, intercessory, etc.

7. I offer for your consideration the following definition of prayer:

Prayer is addressing oneself to God; or to others or
oneself in the presence of God; and consciously
engaging in the interplay of forces.

ᠺᠥ

8. This definition covers prayer with and without
words; contemplation and intercession; the orientation
of the self toward God and the Virgin Mary, the Saints
and the holy Angels; addressing others and even
oneself, as in the Psalms, e.g. "When shall I come and
behold the face of God?" (Ps. 42:2) and "Praise the
Lord, O my soul, and all that is within me praise his
holy name!" (Ps. 103:1).

ᠺᠥ

9. I suggest that you read the book right through and
get an overall idea of it. Then you could start to use it, as
you are moved. It cannot be emphasized too strongly
that each person is free to use this, or any such book,
subject to whatever the Lord is teaching him or her. The
freedom of the Spirit is the watchword of prayer.

ᠺᠥ

10. This means that you can omit, modify or substitute
as you wish, but at the same time having regard, if you
will, to the character and principles of the book.

ᠺᠥ

Abba

Principles and Leading Themes

11. The author of *The Cloud of Unknowing* recommends the use of few words in prayer: "the fewer the better. If it is a little word of one syllable, I think it is better than if it is of two", and he explains that the earnest cry of "this short little prayer of one syllable" pierces heaven "because it is prayed with a full heart".*

༖

12. This teaching corresponds with the Gospels and the economy of the Lord's Prayer itself; and is in the spirit of the Psalms, which abound in short and forceful expressions of prayer.

༖

13. This is the Eastern Orthodox doctrine of "monologic prayer," literally the "prayer of one word"* which, however, can be any short prayer, especially if it is frequently repeated, and during medieval times came to be applied specifically to the "Jesus Prayer" formula (see **56**).

༖

14. So Abbot Isaac says: "We should . . . make short but frequent prayers"*, and the Rule of St Benedict states: "Our prayer should be pure and short".*

༖

15. The authentic tradition links brevity of expression with frequency of repetition, e.g. the Russian Orthodox "Pilgrim" recommends unceasing prayer and makes the interesting observation: "God has assigned to the will and strength of man only the *quantity* of prayer . . . frequency of prayer is his own, and within the province of his will."* He speaks in particular of the Jesus Prayer.

༒

16. In the West, it was said of the saintly English Carmelite William Sothfeld (d. 1414) that he offered the Hail Mary a thousand times a day.* It seems to me that this great prayer of the Western Church corresponds, in many ways, to the Jesus Prayer of the East.

༒

17. I am not saying that we should all follow the example of the Pilgrim and William Sothfeld! But their practice can be borne in mind; and many people may find themselves drawn to frequent recitation of a short prayer-formula.

༒

18. This leads naturally to the idea of the *mantra*. This is "a Sanskrit term used in Hinduism signifying a sacred word, verse or syllable which embodies in sound some specific deity or supernatural power."* This is not exactly the same as the "little word" of *The Cloud* but the following words of Raimundo Panikkar may provide a fruitful connection. He speaks of "*shabdabrahman* (God-word)": "To acquire the energy of the word, one has to grasp not only its meaning but also its message and its vibrations . . . Faith, understanding and physical utterance, as well as physical continuity . . . are essential requisites for an authentic mantra . . .".*

༒

19. We have now arrived at the idea of a "God-word" or prayer-word – and the series of single words used in the exercise described in this book are meant to be such, even though several of them do not have that character of themselves. The spirit of the exercise is meant to be that of the teachings referred to in the foregoing paragraphs **11–18**.

༡

20. Authentic Christian devotion is Trinitarian in character, and this is the intention of the exercise.

༡

21. Prayer should be an integrative act, bringing together the whole self, body, mind and spirit or heart; as Eckhart says, "Be one, in order that you may find God."* We could put it another way: find God or be found by God, and you will become one.

༡

22. The exercise brings together elements from different spiritual traditions and religions, especially Hindu Yoga, but also Buddhism and Taoism.

༡

23. As will be already apparent, the exercise also links two great Christian traditions, of East and West. This is in line with a widespread tendency in recent years.

༡

24. I have in mind also the linking of male and female elements in each of us. The integration of the whole self (see **21**) requires this. Creativity implies male plus female, and prayer is a creative activity; it is the work of the *Creator Spiritus*, the creative Holy Spirit.

༡

25. Finally, under the heading of integration, we can note the words of the Sri Lankan theologian, Tissa Balasuriya, who speaks of the "integrated spirituality" required by the "planetary age" in which we live, which has three norms: individual and personal sanctity; sanctity mediated through an institution ("a community or a church"); and "sanctity as the search for the kingdom of God." "The planetary age requires an integrated spirituality in which all three norms converge in the direction of a personal conscience and a community (authority) urging us towards the common good of humanity."*

26. Since the method of prayer-words involves linking them with yogic breathing and body-centres (see **38–47**) it is important to note the principle and character which underlie the various forms of Yoga. "Etymologically, *yoga* derives from the root *yuj*, 'to bind together', 'hold fast', 'yoke'" (Mircea Eliade).* "The word YOGA comes from the root Yuj which means to join, and in its spiritual sense, it is that process by which the human spirit is brought into near and conscious communion with, or is merged in, the Divine Spirit" (Sivananda).* The classic exposition of Patanjali begins with the statement that Yoga is "the control of thought-waves in the mind,"* or, in Fr Slade's translation, "a technique for the mastery of mental images."*

27. It will be clear that this book owes much to the Orthodox teaching about the Prayer of the Heart, meaning prayer which takes place at, and proceeds from, the very centre of one's being. To achieve that prayer is, in one sense, the object of the whole exercise.

28.   The prayer of *one word*, set out in this book, takes its place between the prayer with *words and images* and the prayer *without words and images*. The ultimate is silent, imageless prayer, when a person is lost in God; and the blank pages at the end of the Main Exercise are meant to suggest that goal. But, of course, we cannot, and should not try to, force the pace. It is up to the Holy Spirit and the will of God. Our part is to aspire, watch and wait upon the Lord. We have the end in view, which is not a spiritual state but God; and most of us will have to wait until the next life before that union is fully realized.

℘

29.   The method of this book can be seen as a practical exercise in the *apophatic* way of prayer, which is a process of affirming and then passing beyond positive ideas and images of God towards the divine reality itself "when, in the presence of God, speech and thought fail us and we are reduced to silence" (Andrew Louth, on "apophatic theology").* This process cannot be carried through by our own will and effort. We can seek and desire, but it is divine grace which grants the contemplation of God in adoring silence.

℘

30.   The whole of prayer, from beginning to end, is a co-operative enterprise between human desire and effort, and divine grace, beautifully expressed in the words of the prophet:

Let us know, let us press on to know the Lord; his going forth is sure as the dawn; he will come to us as the showers, as the spring rains that water the earth (Hos. 6:3).

℘

19

life
light
love

The Method

31. This book describes a single exercise of meditative prayer – the "Prayer Words" (see **57** onwards). It consists of saying (silently, in the mind) a series of prayer-words (see **11–19**). Each word is said to one of the three phases of breathing – out, in, hold (see **38–45**).

In other words, as you breathe out, then in, then hold your breath gently, at each of these three phases you offer one prayer-word and connect it in your mind with one body-centre (see **46**). It sounds a bit complicated but if you decide to use this method (you do not have to, of course, but can work out your own) you will find it is really quite simple, once you have got the hang of it. For easy reference, there is a complete list of prayer-words with breathing marks on the last page-opening of the book.

You can see that this method is in line with the idea of the integration of the whole self in prayer (see **21**): you are using body, mind and spirit together.

32. Under the heading of each prayer-word (beginning with RUAH at **62**) there are some notes and quotations. *These are not meant to be read while you are praying: you read them through beforehand.* When you come to the prayer-word you may recall some of the comments on it (or others which you have discovered yourself) but that is not the important thing. The reading is preliminary and in the background. Just offer each prayer-word to God together with the attention you give to the breath and the body-centre. Make it a simple unified offering to God.

33. This, and other methods and techniques, are human schemes to help us to pray. They cannot do what only the grace of God can do. Real, genuine prayer depends on the Holy Spirit, our teacher and helper (Rom. 8:26–7). So, within the exercise itself, you will see that there is a constant refrain: ABBA (Father) and RUAH (Spirit). The "missing person" of the Trinity is the Son. But that is you, a daughter or son of God, united by faith with Jesus Christ the Son of God who dwells within us (Col. 1:27).

> God has sent the Spirit of his Son into our hearts crying Abba, Father! (Gal. 4:6).

34. How often you use the exercise is up to you. Some may feel that the repetition of prayer-words, many of which have massive content, brings the danger of familiarity breeding contempt. This is always a problem, e.g. with the daily recitation of the Lord's Prayer. We have to live with it and try and overcome it. But you can use the exercise infrequently if you wish, although it might be a good idea to use it on a regular basis.

35. Some of the prayer-words are poetic or mythological. "Myth is . . . the poetic expression of a mystical experience. Myths can only be understood as poetry. They spring from the depths where man encounters the ultimate Mystery of existence and interprets it in poetic form" (Bede Griffiths).*

36. Some of the prayer-words originate in other religions. Probably only two will bother some Christians: KUNDALINI (**104**–7) and OM (**165**–8). If that is the case you can supply another prayer-word yourself, preferably choosing one that fits in, e.g. for KUNDALINI you could have MARY or CHRIST (thought of as *Mother*: see **76**); for OM you could substitute THREE-IN-ONE, the Trinity.

37. The majority of the prayer-words are foreign. I find that a single forceful foreign word compresses and expresses a lot of meaning and it also has a slightly mysterious effect, suggesting the numinous or holy. But it is open to anyone to prefer and use all English! It is interesting, all the same, that the Aramaic word ABBA was preserved in the texts of the New Testament (Mark 14:36; Rom 8–15; Gal. 4:6) along with the Greek translation. This may be explained by its special association with the Prayer of Jesus himself, in the original tongue; but I wonder if there is another sentiment as well, a feeling that the use of such a word helps us to break out of familiar thought-patterns and be more open to divine influence (see **18** on the *mantra*).

38. The science of yogic breathing is called *pranayama*. "Prana is not exactly breath. It is the name for the energy that is in the universe. Whatever you see in the universe, whatever moves or works, or has life, is the manifestation of this Prana" (Vivekananda).* "Breath is the external manifestation of Prana" (Sivananda).* "The process by which the Prana is controlled by regulation of external breath is termed Pranayama" (Sivananda).* According to Tantric Yoga "Breathing is itself a Mantra, known as the Mantra which is not recited" (A. Avalon).*

ℊ

39. There are many complicated forms of pranayama. A simple form, which I recommend, is described by Sivananda: "Inhale slowly and steadily with a concentrated mind. Retain it as long as you can do it comfortably. Then exhale slowly. There should be *no strain* in any stage of Pranayama" (my italics).*

ℊ

40. This is the normal pattern of breathing: in – hold – out. But there is abundant evidence, from a variety of sources, that we should view the pattern differently. This is explained in **41**, together with the yogic names for the three phases, which are used together with the English indications: "Breathe out", "Hold breath", "Breathe in", in the Main Exercise (see **62–186**), and supported by quotations in **42–4**.

41. "When the breath is expired, it is RECHAKA, the first kind of Pranayama. When the breath is drawn in, it is the second, termed PURAKA. When it is suspended, it is the third kind, called KUMBHAKA. Kumbhaka is the retention of breath" (Sivandanda).*

ℊ

42. The Russian Orthodox "Pilgrim" is told: "Sit down alone and in silence. Lower your head, shut your eyes, *breathe out gently*, and imagine yourself looking into your own heart . . . As you breathe out, say, 'Lord Jesus Christ, have mercy on me'" (my italics).* This is one form of the Jesus Prayer (see **56**).

43. Zen: "The technique therefore begins by encouraging a full release of the breath – *easing it out* . . . The returning in-breath is then allowed to follow as a simple reflex action" (Alan Watts; my italics).*

44. Medical testimony: "Breathing out is the more important movement and is longer, breathing in is 'unimportant'" (Dr Barbara Brosnan).*

45. A further important point about breathing is that we should try and learn to breathe deeply (but always without strain) from the abdomen.

46. In Yoga there are six body-centres called *chakras* with a seventh at the top of the head. Some of these correspond to the four centres of concentration and prayer identified by some authors in the Hesychastic tradition of the Eastern Orthodox Church.* *Chakras* – literally "circles" or "discs" or "wheels" – "are called the knots or centres and are sometimes represented as lotuses" (Alain Daniélou).* They are located around the spinal cord: at the base of the spine, the root of the sex organ, the belly, the heart, the throat, and between the eyebrows. The seventh, at the crown of the head, is called *sahasrara* = thousand, the "thousand-petalled lotus." These body-centres may be understood symbolically or mythologically (see **35**) but in any case their significance and their affinity with certain Biblical images will be apparent.

℘

47.   The main exercise of this book, then, incorporates these seven centres in an "ascending" series, as will be seen. The structure of the human body itself is employed to facilitate an "ascending" movement of prayer. But the words of a great twelfth-century writer will keep the programme and the pictorial imagery in perspective:

> Thus, when speaking of spiritual and unseen things, something is said to be "the highest", it is said to be so not as if it were in some place above the topmost peak of heaven, but as deepest of all within us. To ascend to God means, therefore, to enter into oneself, and not only to enter into oneself, but in some ineffable manner to penetrate even into one's depths. He, then, who, if I may so say, enters really deeply into himself and, penetrating deep within, transcends himself, he of a truth ascends to God . . . .

(Hugh of St Victor)*

℘

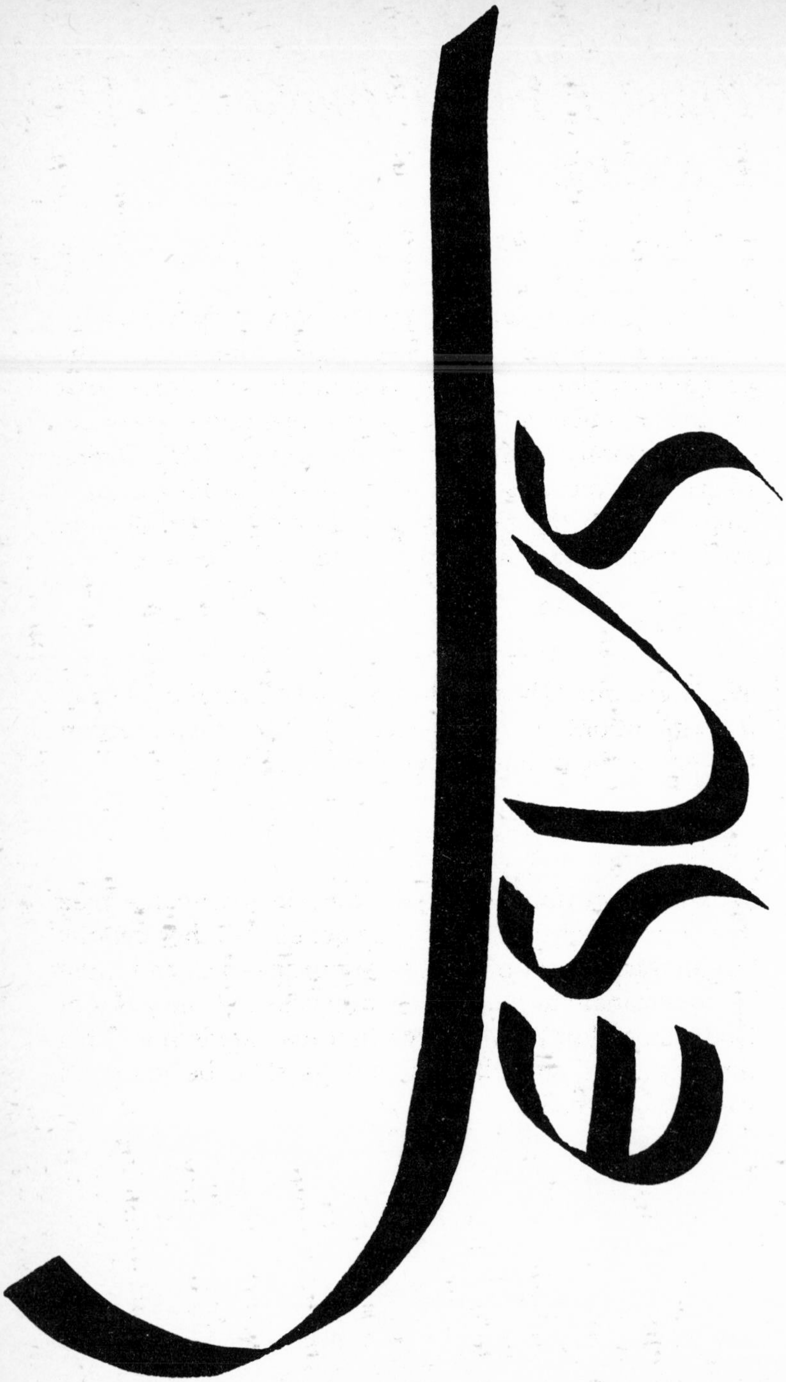

Phase I: Preliminary Exercise

48. St Ignatius taught us the vital importance of beginning prayer with the right intention: "The preparatory prayer is to ask God our Lord for grace that all my intentions, actions, and operations may be ordered purely to the service and praise of His Divine Majesty." And this is so fundamental to his Spiritual Exercises that the same prayer should be made before every meditation "without change."*

ॐ

49. In Islam, "The worshipper must form the 'Niyyat' (i.e. intention) in his or her mind of the particular Prayer . . . he or she is about to offer."*

ॐ

50. We pray for several reasons, including the true development of the self and the benefit of other people; but all these lesser intentions are included in and must be subordinate to the supreme objective of the glory of God; as our Lord says, "seek first his kingdom and his righteousness and all these things shall be yours as well" (Matt. 6:33).

ॐ

51. With this general teaching in mind, you can choose how you express your intention and ask for the Holy Spirit to help you. I usually dedicate the exercise to the Sacred Heart of Jesus; to the glory of the Blessed Trinity; and in honour of and asking the prayers of the Virgin Mary, the Saint of the day (if applicable), St Raphael (angel of healing and journeys) and my Guardian Angel.

ഗ്ന

52. I find it very helpful and satisfying to go through some yogic postures in conjunction with offering the Hail Mary (see **55**), the Jesus Prayer (see **56**), short prayers from the Psalms, etc. This has the effect of stretching and "warming up" mind and body, in preparation for the main exercise.

ഗ്ന

53. Whether or not you want to follow that practice, I do strongly recommend one simple posture, for any prayer exercise, including this one. You sit on your heels, with the soles of your feet turned up; with back, neck and head straight; and hands resting on your knees. This is called *vajrasana* and according to Swami Sivananda, "This is the most common Asana (= posture) . . . Yogins generally sit in this Asana."* He also says that it "resembles more or less the Namaz pose in which Moslems sit for prayer." It is used by Buddhists and is also associated with the Carmelite order in the Church. This makes it very ecumenical in character which should commend it to all of us. It is very prayerful and physically solid and stable. If you should find the posture distractingly uncomfortable, you can use a folding stool called a seiza bench, which is fully described in a recent book by Martin Smith.*

ഗ്ന

54. Sitting in this posture, you may like to practise the *brahma mudra* which is turning the head to the right, then to the left, then up and finally down. You can pray for other people (on your "right" and on your "left"), "look up" to God in praise and petition, and down into your own heart, united with the Sacred Heart of Jesus (see **42**).

❧

55. The text of the Hail Mary is: Hail Mary full of grace, the Lord is with thee. Blessed art thou among women and blessed is the fruit of thy womb, Jesus. Holy Mary, Mother of God, pray for us sinners now and at the hour of our death.

❧

56. The text of the Jesus Prayer of the Orthodox Church is (with authentic variants): Lord Jesus Christ, Son of (the living) God, have mercy on me (us) (a sinner).

❧

truth

Phase II: Main Exercise:
The Prayer Words

57.   First, the question of posture. St Ignatius, with his usual liberality, allows for various bodily postures for "contemplation" even including "lying face upwards"!* Patanjali, in the *Yoga Sutras*, simply says posture must be "firm and pleasant."* Richard Rolle, the fourteenth-century English mystic, decided: "if I were to hold on to and retain deep devotion I must sit . . . if the philosopher (i.e. Aristotle) is right, it is the quiet sitting that makes the soul wise."* And in our own day, Robert Llewelyn refers to the Zen word *shikantaza* – literally "just sitting."*

ᛰ

58.   Whether you stand, sit (on the ground or in a chair), sit in *vajrasana* (see **53**) or kneel, there is one point on which there is a wide consensus: "Holding the body, head, and neck erect, immovably steady" (*Bhagavat Gita*)* – but, of course, without tension or strain.

ᛰ

59. As mentioned above (**31**) each prayer-word of the exercise is linked to one of the three breath-movements – Rechaka, Puraka and Kumbhaka (see **41**). This is in the spirit of St Ignatius' "third method of prayer" in the *Spiritual Exercises*:

> With each breath of respiration prayer may be made mentally, saying one word of the Our Father, or of any other prayer that is being recited, in such a way that only one word is said between one breath and another; and in the time between one breath and another let attention be specially paid to the meaning of that word, or to the Person whom one is addressing . . .*.

ᶜᵖ

60. So, in a steady and comfortable posture, you begin the exercise by breathing out gently (*Rechaka*) and asking for the Holy Spirit, e.g. *Veni Creator Spiritus*. Come Creator Spirit (see **30**, **33** and **48**).

ᶜᵖ

61. Now, with the in-breath (*Puraka*) you begin the first prayer-word RUAH. It so happens that the sixty "words" of the exercise tally with the sixty "items" on the traditional Catholic rosary: fifty-nine beads plus the crucifix. If you have a rosary and wanted to use your hands to finger-count your way through, you could certainly do so; although there is a lot to be said for keeping the hands at rest and quite still.

The complete sequence of prayer words with their breathing marks can be found on pp. 118–119.

ᶜᵖ

62. The Hebrew word RUAH in the Old Testament has the sense of wind/breath/spirit/divine power/breath of life, and especially the "life-giving breath or power of God in men and animals" (Gesenius).* For Hindus, from the time of the ancient Vedic hymns, there was a correspondence between breath and the "cosmic wind."* For Christians, RUAH refers especially to the Holy Spirit, the Lord, the Giver of Life; creative, dynamic, penetrating.

ॐ

63. The Spirit of God "was moving over the face of the waters" at the Creation, according to Genesis 1:2.

ॐ

64. St Paul tells us (and the experience of countless Christians testifies) that the Spirit helps us to pray (Rom. 8:26–7) and "searches everything, even the depths of God" (1 Cor. 2:10), and therefore the depths of each of us creatures.

ॐ

65. Bede Griffiths believes that "The Spirit is the feminine principle in the Godhead, the Mother of all creation. It is in her that the seeds of the Word are planted and she nurtures them and brings them forth in creation."* This belief has support within the ancient tradition of the Church, as the Doctrine Commission of the Church of England points out in its 1987 Report:

> In the early Syriac theology and in the Pseudo-Macarian homilies . . . the Spirit is feminine and motherly.*

Whether or not we subscribe to that belief, it can only be right to have a strong sense of the creative, enabling, nurturing grace of the Holy Spirit.

ॐ

66. "Awake, awake, put on strength, O arm of the Lord!" (Isa. 51:9); "Awake, awake, put on your strength, O Zion!" (Isa. 52:1). I ask the Lord within me to rise up, to rouse me, to stir up my sleepy soul; and I call on myself to cooperate actively with the inward grace of the Holy Spirit, to "rekindle the gift of God that is within" us (2 Tim. 1:6).

<p>

67. "Now the grace of God, pouring forth from God, is an inward thrust and urge of the Holy Ghost, driving forth our spirit from within . . . for God is more inward to us than we are to ourselves, and His inward thrust or working within us, be it natural or supernatural, is nearer to us and more intimate to us, than our own working is. And therefore God works in us from within outwards; but all creatures work from without inwards" (Ruysbroeck).*

<p>

68. "Jesus sleeps spiritually in your heart, as He once did in the body when He was in the ship with his disciples. But they, fearing to perish, wakened Him and He quickly saved them from the storm. In the same way do you rouse Him by prayer and waken Him with the cry of your desire, and He will quickly arise and help you" (Walter Hilton).*

<p>

69. "Awake, O my soul, awake, and arise from the dust, and come before the Lord thy God" (St Gertrude).*

"Arise, my soul; arise out of the dust, thou captive daughter of Sion. Arise, forsake the puddle of thy negligent life. Return unto the Lord thy God, for he expecteth thee. Make haste, be not slack, for He is ready to receive thee" (Augustine Baker).*

"Awake! awake O sleeper of the land of shadows, wake! Expand! I am in you and you in me, mutual in love divine" (William Blake).*

"The word Buddha comes from the root BUDH, to be awake, to be conscious of, to know," and: "The followers of Buddha Gotama are awake and for ever watch".*

ჟ

awake

70. AB*BA* (accent on the second syllable as in the sound of the Islamic holy name, All*ah*) is the Aramaic word for *father* "used in prayer . . . and in the family circle".* It has an intimate feel and as an address to God with the meaning "my Father" or (almost) "dada" it seems to have orginated with Jesus, to be characteristic of his own usage and a special grace granted to those who believe in him (see Rom. 8:15; Gal. 4:6).

⌒

71. This word, in the time of Jesus "an everyday word, a homely family-word",* but used by him to address the King of heaven, was given to his disciples and so to us: "the giving of the Lord's Prayer to the disciples authorized them to say 'Abba', just as Jesus did. In this way, Jesus gave them a share in his relationship with God" (Joachim Jeremias).*

⌒

72. An Orthodox writer says: "Likewise a mother teaches her child the word 'dada' by repeating it with him until he has got into the way of calling for his father with confidence, even in sleep."*

⌒

73. The question arises: how to reconcile the masculine gender of "Father" both with the fact that the infinite and eternal Godhead must embrace and go beyond male and female, and with the growing feminist consciousness which is making legitimate demands upon the language and thought-patterns, liturgy, theology and devotion of the Church? In **74–78** I offer some observations on this matter.

⌒

74. ABBA, because of its childlike character (see **72**) could be regarded as virtually sexless, 'dada', a *parent*-name.

℘

75. On the idea of the Holy Spirit as "the feminine principle in the Godhead", see **65**.

℘

76. The Lord Jesus Christ manifests in the Gospels (especially the Fourth) very strong female as well as male features, with several striking mothering-images of feeding, nourishing, etc. This led, in the Middle Ages, to the development of devotion to Christ as our Mother, especially in St Anselm and Julian of Norwich. "For longing to bear sons into life, you tasted death, and by dying you begot them. So you, Lord God, are the great Mother" (St Anselm).* "Jesus Christ is our real Mother. We owe our being to him – and this is the essence of motherhood! . . . Our beloved Mother, Jesus, feeds us with himself . . . our tender Mother Jesus simply leads us into his blessed breast through his open side . . ." (Julian of Norwich).*

℘

77. Bede Griffiths says about the "abyss of the Godhead": "Jesus himself knew it as Abba, Father, but it can also be called the Mother. The Hindu knows it as both Father and Mother . . . We need to know it as both Mother and Father."* The Sikh Arjan (d. 1606) says: "Even if I have gone astray, I am thy child, O God; thou art my Father and Mother." "I, the Father of this universe, the Mother, the Supporter" (Gita).* And Julian of Norwich: "God is really our Mother as he is our Father."*

℘

78. It seems then, that this refrain ABBA, dada, which, with RUAH, recurs frequently and regularly throughout the sequence of prayer-words, can be used in freedom of the Spirit, by men and women of diverse persuasions, and without the disturbing pressure of gender-based assumptions. Whatever your views, the one thing necessary is surely to use this loving gift of the Lord with a deep sense of the gracious privilege of thus addressing the one who is the "fount, source and origin of all."

ᠬ

RUAH   *Breathe in*   (*Puraka*)   See **62–65**

Abba

79. "How sweet the name of Jesus sounds, in a believer's ear" and how rich and profound are the sentiments aroused by this holy and saving name. But let us turn first to the one instance recorded in the Gospels where someone addresses the Lord simply as "Jesus", without any addition, rather than "master" or "rabbi", etc. This is the word of the penitent thief to Jesus on the Cross (Luke 23:42). As I repeat the holy name I put myself in the place of that sinner. I speak to Jesus as my friend and brother, one who is alongside me, at my level. But I turn to him as more than a fellow-sufferer (though that is wonderful enough): he is the one who in the end ("when you come into your kingdom") will save me and all of us.

ᡐ

80. "Jesus" means "saviour" (Matt. 1:21); it was an ordinary human name; now it is the Holy Name. He was "the Saviour of the world" (John 4:42) and bore the saving name. He was a human being like us, and bore an ordinary man's name. All this, and many more treasures, are contained in the name of Jesus.

ᡐ

81. There were thousands of crosses and crucifixions in the days of the Roman Empire. For us there is now only one. But it stands for those anonymous thousands with whom Jesus was identified in his crucifixion; and for the millions who have been and are "crucified" since then and in our own day.

ᡐ

82. In the Gospels, this word was also uttered by a penitent, and by a blind beggar. St Mary Magdalene was a penitent, like the thief on the cross, but also a devoted disciple, and she was addressing the risen Lord. So now, I turn from Jesus on the Cross to Jesus risen from the dead (John 20:16).

☞

83. The word comes from the Aramaic and means "my lord" or "my master". It is close in meaning to the respectful form of address (which also became a title) "rabbi"; but it is more intense and personal, especially in this context. However, the evangelist's own translation ("which means Teacher") does have a neutral sound. The only other use of this form of address in the Gospels is very significant: it is by the blind beggar Bartimaeus, sitting by the roadside and calling out, "Jesus, Son of David, have mercy on me!" (Mark 10:47, 51; see also the Jesus Prayer: **56**).

☞

84. There is a certain family likeness between the thief on the cross, the saint who was healed of "seven demons" (Luke 8:2) and this blind beggar. I need to place myself alongside them, as a sinner in need of healing and help. I recall too another cry of intense personal faith and devotion, by the apostle Thomas, also addressed to the risen Lord: "My Lord and my God!" (John 20:28).

☞

85. RABBONI is the response of the disciple to the Master who has called us: "Come to me . . . Take my yoke upon you, and learn from me. . . ." (Matt. 11:28–9). "Yoke" recalls "yoga" (see **26**), so this word links me with both the Jewish teaching tradition of the rabbis (of which Jesus, on earth, was one) and with the idea of Jesus as *guru*, especially in view of the original meaning of the word: "the syllable 'gu' means darkness, the syllable 'ru' means dispeller; he is therefore called a 'guru' because he dispells darkness."*

સ્

86. The teaching and training process of Jesus is founded upon love, the love of the Sacred Heart: "learn from me; for I am gentle and lowly in heart" (Matt. 11:29).

સ્

87. And the response of Christ to Mary Magdalene's cry, the message she is to convey to the other disciples is: "I am ascending to my Father and your Father, to my God and your God" (John 20:17). The essence of the training of Jesus our Master is that he is leading us, not *to* himself, but *through* himself (the "door": John 10:7–10, and the "way": John 14:6) to the Father, to God, beyond all, into the Godhead.

સ્

RUAH *Breathe in* (*Puraka*) See **62–65**

88. This is the Pali (language of the Buddhist scriptures) term meaning "Mindfulness" or "Right Mindfulness" and is the key to Buddhist meditation. It is a combination of two words, meaning attention or awareness; and "placing near (one's mind), i.e. keeping present, remaining aware, establishing."* In Buddhist teaching there are three stages: simple attention, taking notice; sustained and deeper attention; pure, clear concentrated attention.

☙

89. "Mindfulness is the awareness of what one is doing while one is doing it, and of nothing else."* The relevance and importance of this in prayer is obvious. It connects with an important strand of Christian teaching, exemplified by the eighteenth-century Jesuit, Jean-Pierre de Caussade, with his stress on "the sacrament of the present moment";* and with Martin Buber's "full acceptance of the present."* Eckhart even defined prayer as: "the practice of pure being and glorying therein."*

☙

90. In Buddhism the process of becoming wholly present in the present is meant to bring home the futility or vanity of the self, which has no real existence. So, while Christians may gratefully learn about the technique, we respectfully part company with Buddhists when it comes to the end-in-view: instead, the realization of the self in the present moment becomes the gateway to reality, to God.

☙

ABBA   *Breathe out*   (*Rechaka*)   See 70–78

RUAH   *Breathe in*   (*Puraka*)   See 62–65

COGITO   *Hold breath*   (*Kumbhaka*)

91.   COGITO (Latin "I think") stands for Descartes' famous statement "Cogito ergo sum." The philosopher explained (1670): "by the term *thought (cogitatio, pensée)* I comprehend all that is in us, so that we are immediately conscious of it." A.D. Lindsay comments: *"Thought* is thus but another term for *consciousness."** It represents part of the great Hindu triad *sat-chit-ananda* (being – consciousness – bliss) which Abhishiktananda summarized as "my being, my awareness of being, and my joy in being."*

༄

92.   It is not necessary, in order to use this prayer-word, to subscribe to, or even understand or know about the philosophical system of Descartes. The word is, in a sense, an aspect of *satipatthana* (see **88–90**): I am conscious and self-conscious, therefore I (must, at least) exist; and the fact of my existence, and the activity of my conscious mind, is to be ordered towards truth, i.e. God (see **95–8**). This is part of that total worship of God with "the mind" commanded by the Lord (Mark 12:30).

༄

93. An alternative prayer-word could be DENKEN (German "to think"). This was a key concept for Albert Schweitzer, and James Brabazon explains that, besides "thought", it carried "other connotations of meditation, of brooding absorption in a subject, which the word 'thought' does not encompass."*

94. The following poem by D. H. Lawrence, entitled "Thought", was quoted by J. Middleton Murray, following Brabazon, who says it expresses "precisely" what Schweitzer meant by *denken*:

Thought, I love thought.
But not the jiggling and twisting of already existent
ideas.
I despise that self-important game.
Thought is the welling up of unknown life into
consciousness,
Thought is the testing of statements on the
touchstone of the conscience,
Thought is gazing on the face of life, and reading
what can be read,
Thought is pondering over experience, and coming to
a conclusion.
Thought is not a trick, or an exercise, or a set of
dodges,
Thought is a man in his wholeness wholly attending.*

95. "Certainly, when we use the name 'God', one thing we must mean by that name is truth, the final reality that is uncovered when all illusions and errors have been stripped away. The desire for truth implanted in us is the desire to know the real, and 'God' is our name for that which is most real. The desire for truth is the desire for God" (John Macquarrie).*

96. Jesus described his mission thus: "For this I was born . . . to bear witness to the truth" (John 18:37). This is a fundamental statement, like the "God is love" of St John (John 4:8) and it brings out clearly the wide connotation of truth, since Jesus obviously did not devote himself entirely to teaching: his bearing witness to the truth embraced his whole life and actions and, supremely, his sufferings and crucifixion, as well as his words; indeed, he could embody the truth in his own person: "I am . . . truth" (John 14:6).

97.   Mahatma Gandhi said: "God is truth . . . But two years ago I advanced a step further and said that Truth is God. For even the atheists do not doubt the necessity for the power of truth. In their passion for discovering the truth, the atheists have not hesitated to deny the existence of God, and, from their point of view, they are right."* And Meister Eckhart said: "Truth is something so noble that if God could turn aside from it, I could keep to the truth and let God go."*

℘

98.   The first verse of John Masefield's poem "The Ship of Death" reads:

Man with his burning soul
has but an hour of breath
to build a ship of truth
in which his soul may sail
sail on the sea of death.
For death takes toll
of beauty, courage, youth
of all but truth.

℘

RUAH   *Breathe in*   *(Puraka)*   See **62–65**

MULADHARA   *Hold breath*   *(Kumbhaka)*

99.   As you hold your breath for a moment, saying MULADHARA, you concentrate on the *chakra* (see **46**) of that name, which is located at the base of the spine, between the "root" of the genital organ and the anal orifice. MULADHARA is a Sanskrit word meaning "holder of the root" or "root-support" or "supporting root".

℘

100.   This is the area of my seat, my bottom, the place of excretion. It supports my spine and trunk. It represents my physical and chemical base. I am a lowly creature. I have my seat on earth. I sit like other animals and, like them, excrete.

101.   At the same time, this is the base of my spinal column, which reaches up to the brain and all the complexity of the central nervous system.

102.   The yogis believe that in this *chakra* KUNDALINI (see **104–107**) sleeps, symbol of innate divine energy which must be roused, stirred up (see **66–69**) and so energize the whole being.

103.   So I meditate on my basic identity as a human being, a member of a biological species, created by God.

ABBA   *Breathe out*   *(Rechaka)*   See **70–78**

RUAH   *Breathe in*   *(Puraka)*   See **62–65**

104. As you hold your breath for a moment, saying KUNDALINI, you concentrate on the latent energy, the "life-force" (Ernest Wood), which the yogis picture at the base of the spine, the *muladhara chakra*, in "the form of a snake . . . a goddess . . . an energy" (Mircea Eliade).* Kundalini is "the 'cosmic energy'. . . coiled, serpent-fashion" (Déchanet).* It is "Mother Kundalini" (Sivananda). It must be awakened, roused up, so that its "potential energy" (Wood) rises up through the *chakras*, energizing them en route, up to the apex, *sahasrara* (see **46**), where she is united in mystic union, a spiritual marriage, with the god Siva.

ᡐ

105. This imagery finds an echo in Jung's concept of the *libido*, as interpreted by Jim Garrison:

> The central energy, which Jung termed *libido* and referred to as the "unfathomable ground," permeates all sectors of psychic life, remaining essentially unchanged, whatever stratum it energizes. As defined by Jacobi, this central energy is "the total force which pulsates through all the forms and activities of the psychic system and establishes a communication between them."*

ᡐ

106. The innate divine power symbolized by Kundalini can be thought of, in Christian terms, either as that image of God which is "natural" to humankind through God's creation; or as the grace of Baptism whereby the "character" of Christ is, so to speak, implanted in us; or indeed as a union of natural and supernatural grace. In any case, I think it is congruous with both the Kundalini image and the tradition of biblical and Christian spirituality, from the Song of Songs onward, to see the deep spiritual base or "soul" of a person as *female*, as a bride seeking the Bridegroom. In the Christian tradition of mystical theology, the culmination of the "ascent" of the soul to God is the "transforming union" or "spiritual marriage." This mystical state cannot, of course, be induced or produced by human effort – it is the gift of God, absolutely. But sincere and humble aspiration with this end ultimately in view is surely open to every believer; and in receiving Holy Communion, the lowliest Christian is already, in a sense, initiated sacramentally into this state, which should then be realized historically, in this life or the next (and see **68**).

> virgin soul
> virgin heart
> meant for God alone
> seeking God alone
> being found by God
> being formed by God

ᔆ

107. If this imagery is, for any reason, unacceptable to you, you might like to substitute, as background meditation for your prayer, the idea of Motherhood, perhaps using MOTHER as the prayer-word and seeing Christ as our Mother (see **76**) and/or the Virgin Mary as the Mother of Christ and of all Christians (John 19:26–7).

> This fine and lovely word *Mother* is so sweet and so much its own that it cannot properly be used of any but him, and of her who is his own true Mother – and ours.*

You could also reflect on Christ as the "saving serpent": Numbers 21:9 and John 3:14; 8:28; 12:32.

ᔆ

SHEKHI*NAH*   *Breathe out*   *(Rechaka)*

108.   As you gently breathe out and quietly rest for a moment in the emptiness of your lungs, you say SHEKHINAH, a Hebrew word (not biblical but rabbinic) which means, literally, "resting" or "dwelling".

ℛ

109.   In the Jewish religion, it has the sense of the Divine Presence immanent in the world, manifested and located in earthly experience – "a revelation of the holy in the midst of the profane"* – with images associated with light, glory and radiance. In the Jewish mystical system called "the Kabbalah," it is seen as "the daughter, the princess, the feminine principle in the world of the divine *Sefirot*" (= emanations of God).* For Christians, in John 1:14 "and in a number of other passages the word 'glory' (*doxa*) occasionally seems to convey the overtones associated with the Jewish Shekinah."*

ℛ

110.   Here, as a prayer-word, SHEKHINAH can express the sense of Christ dwelling within us (see **106**): "Christ in you the hope of glory" (Col. 1:27); and his presence as a point of departure, from which we ascend, with Christ, through the self to God, from earth to heaven: see the story of Jacob's Ladder (Gen. 28:12; John 1:51) and **47**.

ℛ

RUAH   *Breathe in*   *(Puraka)*   See **62–65**

SVADISHTHANA *Hold breath* (*Kumbhaka*)

111. This *Chakra* – variously translated, from the Sanskrit, "within the self", "centre of self", "support-of-the-life-breath" – is located at the base or root of the male sexual organ. We can take it to refer to the root of the genitalia, male and female, i.e. the basic physical sexual identity.

112. When a baby is born, the first question is: Does it have the basic physical components and functions? The second is: Is it a boy or a girl? Gender is identified by genitalia.

113. As I have reflected, at the *muladhara chakra*, on my identity as a human being, a member of a biological species, so now I reflect on my sexual identity as male or female, and on my sexual orientation. These are essential to the rootedness of my being.

114. However a person is orientated sexually, and whether sexuality is suppressed, expressed or sublimated, this fundamental element of my being must be recognized, affirmed and offered to God; and I need to recognize, affirm and offer, too, that "other" side of my sexuality (male or female) – that which I am not but which is present within me.

ABBA *Breathe out* (*Rechaka*) See **70–78**

RUAH *Breathe in* (*Puraka*) See **62–65**

115. The ancient Chinese couplet is YIN/YANG but I am reversing the order because YIN leads on more naturally to MANIPURA, as will be seen.

༠

116. The couplet represents the male (YANG) and female (YIN) principles of reality and humanity, and the respective attributes are summarized in James Legge's *The Texts of Taoism**:

YANG	YIN
Expansion (breathe in/ hold)	Contraction (breathe out)
Motion/movement	Rest/stillness
Heaven	Earth
Sun	Moon

༠

117. "All things are twofold, one opposite the other, and he has made nothing incomplete. One confirms the good things of the other, and who can have enough of beholding his glory?" (Ecclus 42:24–5).

༠

118. Speaking of "those who know the joy of heaven", Chuang Tzu says: "in their stillness they possess the quality of Yin, and in their movement they flow abroad as the Yang."* He speaks also of the "Perfect Music", "the harmony of the Yin and Yang", comparing it with "the sun and moon". One is reminded that the title of the most popular form of Yoga, Hatha, is usually understood to be a combination of Ha (sun) and Tha (moon); and the main arteries of the "subtle body" in Tantric Yoga are "the Ida artery on the left" corresponding to "the lunar principle", and, "on the right is the Pingala artery, the male shape, the solar principle."*

⌒

119.   Prayer should help to integrate the self (see **21**) and an important part of that process is the harmonizing of the male and female elements within each of us (see **24**), so that whichever is our gender and basic sexual orientation, we recognize and affirm the other side of the self (see **117**). The Freudian analyst Marion Milner, in her book *The Hands of the Living God*, describing the case of "Susan", a severely mentally-ill patient, writes about the drawings which she produced in the course of treatment:

> the male and female symbols that the oval now contains could stand for a dawning idea that the core of the self is not a "thing" but a process, an interplay of pure being and awareness of being.* (see **91**)

and Dr Milner refers to the psycho-analytical idea that

> psychic health seems to be conceived of, unconsciously, as a state in which the two parents are felt to be in creative intercourse within the psyche.* (see **24**)

⌒

120.   So now, as I gently hold my breath for a moment, saying YANG, I meditate on the active, outward, extrovert aspect of my life.

⌒

RUAH   *Breathe in*   *(Puraka)*   See **62–65**

121. And as I gently breathe out, saying YIN, I meditate on the contemplative, inward, introverted aspect of my life.

122. YIN is the Holy Saturday of the self, the phase of the womb, of the seed growing secretly; of the tomb preparing for the emergence of resurrection life; recalling the Virgin Mary, in whose womb Jesus was conceived and brought to birth, who "kept all these things, pondering them in her heart" (Luke 2:19); and that other Mary "who sat at the Lord's feet and listened to his teaching," choosing the "one thing needful" (Luke 10:39, and **42**).

RUAH *Breathe in* *(Puraka)* See **62–65**

MANIPURA   *Hold breath*   *(Kumbhaka)*

123.   The *Manipura chakra* is located in the belly. The Sanskrit word means "city of jewels" and so suggests *riches* in the depths of one's being.

ᴖ

124.   Coupling it with the "twin" word KOILIA (see **126–131**), the focus here can be on the *natural* resources and riches which are present within a person, by virtue of creation by God through the parents. Marion Milner (see **119**) says of her patient "Susan" that she needed to:

> hold herself and *live from her own middle*, come down from her head and from trying to hold herself up by her head, come down to an acceptance of her head as balanced on, held up by, the whole body, including the upright spine and sense of weight upon what supports the body* (my italics).

ᴖ

125.   These natural resources, e.g. the autonomous defence-systems of the body which resist invasive bacteria and promote healing, and the astonishing mental powers displayed by "ordinary" people in the face of crushing life-experiences (poverty, disease, bereavement, torture, etc.) are grounds for deep and humble thankfulness and also confidence in one's own God-given capacity for coping with the vicissitudes of life.

ᴖ

ABBA   *Breathe out*   *(Rechaka)*   See **70–78**

RUAH   *Breathe in*   *(Puraka)*   See **62–65**

126.   This Greek word means "belly" or "womb" and occurs several times in the New Testament. It is the organ of digestion and reproduction, the innermost recess of the body, closely associated with the heart (see KARDIA: **140–144**), the deep centre of the self; in fact, the KOILIA is (the "cave") where the KARDIA is found.

ᢀᢏ

127.   As I gently retain my breath, saying KOILIA, I concentrate on the *chakra* (see **46**) of my belly or womb.

ᢀᢏ

128.   "He who believes in me, as the scripture has said, 'Out of his heart (KOILIA) shall flow rivers of living water'" (John 7:38). It is debated whether the reference is to the water of life (Holy Spirit) issuing from the Body of Christ (John 19:34) or (derivatively) from the believer as united with Christ. For devotional purposes, we can have it both ways. Through my union with Christ, who dwells in my heart by faith (Eph. 3:17), I experience the depth of my being as a fruitful well; I bear Christ within me spiritually as the Virgin Mary bore him physically in her womb. I can be creative, fruitful and give birth – to good thoughts, words and works.

ᢀᢏ

129.   The KOILIA is a cavity within the body, and so a cave, a place, a space; recalling the cave of Bethlehem where Christ was born, the cave of Lazarus, and where the Body of Jesus was laid, and the many caves of the Holy Land, where the pilgrim descends into the darkness and secrecy of the rock and the earth; potent symbol of the secret places of the innermost self and of God who dwells in the secret place, the cave of the heart.

᠊ᡴ᠊

130.   The KOILIA symbolizes life-giving union, with Christ and the Virgin Mary, the Mother of Christ and our Mother – in the words of Pope John Paul II, "the spiritual mother of humanity,"* who is also, according to Pope Paul VI, "truly our sister"* and was thus addressed by Friar William Herebert in the fourteenth century: "my sister and mother".*

᠊ᡴ᠊

131.   The navel is also the perpetual sign of my biological connection with my mother, my parents, with the human race. And the belly is my "guts", where fear churns but also courage and fortitude arise, through the natural or supernatural gift of the Holy Spirit.

᠊ᡴ᠊

132. "I am . . . life" (John 14:6): first, existence itself, the fundamental difference between being and not-being; biological, natural life: "In him was life, and the life was the light of men" (John 1:4).

༧

133. But, even more than that: "I came that they may have life, and have it abundantly" (John 10:10). St Irenaeus, quoted by Pope John Paul II, said: "The glory of God is that man should be fully alive."

༧

134. The theme of Life (and Death), fundamental throughout the Bible, has taken on a new meaning in our time through the liberation movement and theology originating in Latin America. Archbishop Oscar Romero of El Salvador, prominent among many champions of the poor and the oppressed, was martyred by an assassin's bullet while saying Mass on 24 March 1980. I was in Mexico in 1988 on the anniversary of his death, and realized that he had already been unofficially canonized by millions of people throughout Latin America. He said:

> We believe in Jesus who came to give life in abundance and we believe in a living God who gives life to human beings, and wants them truly to live. These radical truths of faith become really truths when the Church involves itself in the life and death of its people. So the Church like every person is faced with the most basic option for its faith, being for life or death.*

Frei Betto, the Brazilian Dominican, said:

> For Jesus, the world wasn't divided between the pure and the impure, as the Pharisees wished; it was divided between those who favoured Life and those who supported Death. Everything that generates life – from a gesture of love to social revolution – is in line with God's scheme of things, in line with the construction of the Kingdom, for life is the greatest gift given to us by God.*

135. The Holy Spirit is, in the words of the Creed, "the Lord, the Giver of Life." As we offer this prayer-word, it can be a prayer in the Spirit, through Christ who is Life, to the God of Life: in praise of life, thanksgiving for life; petition for life on behalf of those who are denied it by others, or by their own option for death; for life in all its fulness.

RUAH   *Breathe in*   (*Puraka*)   See **62–65**

136. This Sanskrit word (literally "one-handed") means "unstruck (sound)": "*anahata sabd* is the sound produced without contact between two objects; i.e. a mystical sound" (Eliade).* The yogis say that some people have a consciousness of a perpetual sound, heard within the heart. Of course, this must be carefully distinguished from background humming noises due to external, mechanical causes; and from internal physical disturbances such as "singing in the ears"! Ernest Wood says: "Kundalini lies sleeping in her bulb or cave (*kanda*) at the base of the spine (see **104**) where she has the nature of the *shabda-Brahman*, that is, Brahman operating in form which is primarily sound – meaningful sound."* Arthur Avalon says that the "Western term" for *shabda-Brahman* is "the Logos" (see **137**).*

ᢩᡔ

137.   The Bible sees the origin of creation in the Word (Logos) of God (John 1:1–3). It might be possible to think of this under the imagery of mystical or meaningful sound, emanating from the Godhead. According to Tantric Yoga: "When. . . the time for creation takes place, there is a stirring. . . and an initial vibration . . . known as Cosmic Sound (*Sabda-brahman*)."*

ᢩᡔ

138. There is a silence which has the quality of sound and vice versa. St John of the Cross speaks of "silent music". It is a sort of *continuo* and suggests an abiding ground-base to existence, an image of the divine, as of a voice serenely singing.

ᠭ

139. The prophet Elijah, during his encounter with God in the cave at Mount Horeb, heard a "thin, sighing sound" (1 Kings 19:12). The NEB's "a low murmuring sound" is a better translation here than the common (including CB) but misleading "a still small voice." This could have been "a mystical sound." In any case, this whole wonderful story of 1 Kings 19 provides rich material for meditation, especially as background to this prayer-word and OM (see **165–168**).

ᠭ

ABBA   *Breathe out*   (*Rechaka*)   See **70–78**

RUAH   *Breathe in*   (*Puraka*)   See **62–65**

KARDIA   *Hold breath*   (*Kumbhaka*)

140.   This Greek word means "heart" and it occurs many times in the New Testament. The "cave of the heart" (see **129**) symbolizes the centre of the self, and the place of meeting: between the self and Christ, who may "dwell" there "by faith" (Eph. 3:17) and so with God; and between the unconscious and the conscious; and so it is a place of integration, communion and union. The eighteenth-century Anglican divine, William Law, said:

> Turn to thy heart, and thy heart will find its saviour, its God, within itself . . . Seek for him in thy heart, and thou wilt never seek in vain, for there he dwells, there is the seat of his light and Holy Spirit.*

Here is the heart of the matter and the heart of prayer. Christ is the centre. He occupies the "place" between the Father and the Spirit, between God and Creation, between us and the Trinity. He is the Word, the Mediator, the saving, mediating Word. And here, in my heart, symbolically, mystically, he is the centre of the self, of my being, my life.

ℴ

141. Both the Eastern Orthodox and the Hindus speak of the heart as the centre of the self and a kind of shrine, e.g.

the shrine of your heart, which is closed to every conception derived from the sensible world, that image-free dwelling-place illumined by dispassion (= "state of reintegration and spiritual freedom") and the overshadowing of God's grace (St John of Karthapos).*

Within the city of Brahman, which is the body, there is the heart, and within the heart there is a little house. This house has the shape of a lotus, and within it dwells that which is to be sought after, inquired about, and realized . . . Though old age comes to the body, the lotus of the heart does not grow old. It does not die with the death of the body (Chandogya Upanishad).*

༄

142. The Orthodox *startsi* (saintly spiritual directors) teach that we should shift our "locus" from "the head" to "the heart." This means a shift from meditation and praying with thoughts at a superficial level, to a deeper, more "affective" prayer of communion with God:

You must descend from your head into your heart. To concentrate the mind in the heart means to establish the attention in the heart, and mentally to see before you the ever-present and invisible God" (Theophan the Recluse).*

Compare this with words from the great classic texts of Hinduism, e.g.: "Holding the body steady . . . And causing the senses with the mind to enter the heart . . .",* and "the mind confined in the heart".*

༄

143. Two mystics, one from the fourteenth and one from the twentieth century, share their visions of the Sacred Heart of Jesus Christ, which can be the special form or image consonant with his presence within the human heart; one disclosing it as a place of love and peace, the other as a sign of the whole Christ, his totality and essence, which is Love, the Heart of God, the fire of Love.

With a glad countenance our Lord looked at his side, rejoicing as he gazed. And as I looked, I, with my limited understanding, was led by way of this same wound into his side. There he showed me a place, fair and delightful, large enough for all saved mankind to rest in peace and love (Julian of Norwich).*

How strange, my God, are the processes your Spirit initiates! When, two centuries ago, your Church began to feel the particular power of your heart, it might have seemed that what was captivating men's souls was the fact of their finding in you an element even more determinate, more circumscribed, than your humanity as a whole. But now on the contrary a swift reversal is making us aware that your main purpose in this revealing to us of your heart was to enable our love to escape from the constrictions of the too narrow, too precise, too limited image of you which we had fashioned for ourselves. What I discern in your breast is simply a furnace of fire; and the more I fix my gaze on its ardency the more it seems to me that all around it the contours of your body melt away and become enlarged beyond all measure, till the only features I can distinguish in you are those of the face of a world which has burst into flame (Teilhard de Chardin).*

$\sim$

144. The Sacred Heart is the image of *incarnate* Love: "O most Sacred symbol and sacrament of Love, divine and human, in its fulness" (Cardinal Newman).* And the beauty of it is that it represents Christ both as he *was*, on earth, and as he *is now*, ever leading us to God, the heart of eternal and infinite Love. The union of divine and human in Christ is, according to Jim Garrison in his discussion of Jung, reflected in the depth of the human psyche: "that place within us that is capable of being wholly divine and wholly human simultaneously."* As my unconscious rises up and my conscious mind descends, there can be in the heart a meeting of the self with itself and with the Lord. I find myself, I find the Lord.

145. Breathing out gently, I move directly from
KARDIA to the prayer-word LOVE. "God is love"
(1 John 4:8) is one of the few simple, unequivocal
statements that can be made about God, and the
universal and apostolic testimony in the New Testament is that Love is the "very essence of God" (St
Gertrude), and also constitutes the basic need and
requirement of humankind. This is corroborated empir-
ically by psychological observation throughout the ages
and verified clinically in modern times. The fourteenth-
century writer Richard Rolle said: "To love and be loved
is the delightful purpose of all human life."*

ᦥ

146. All the rich and varied forms of love are
contained in this all-important word – familial and
sexual; friendship and fellowship, natural and supernatural; the love of God for us which makes possible
ours for him (1 John 4:19); our love for other people, for
animals, creatures and things. This prayer-word is an
act of praise and thanksgiving and also an expression of
at least my desire and hope to love; which is the key to
my relationship with God and all others.

ᦥ

147. The fourteenth-century Dominican mystic John
Tauler said:

> For Christ, according to the human nature which he
> had taken on him, was not only a servant, but a
> servant of servants, and served all of us for three and
> thirty years and more in great labour and suffering
> . . . And, indeed, his whole life long he spent in this;
> namely, in inviting all men to his supper. For this he

preached, he worked miracles, he went from place to place, he cried out, and proclaimed that the kingdom of heaven was at hand, and that every man should make ready for it. But they would not come. And when the Father of the household heard this, he said unto his servant: *Compel them to come in, that my house may be filled.* Then that servant thought thus with himself: how shall I be able, by subtlety and without violence, to compel these men to come, that both rebellion may be avoided, and yet the right and faculty of free will may remain to them untouched? For if I compel them to come by chains of iron, and hard blows, and scourges, I shall have asses, not men. He said then within himself: I perceive the condition of man, how he is given to love. Therefore I will show him such love as shall pass all his understanding, nay, than which none can be greater. Now if man will observe this, he will feel himself so caught fast in its meshes, that he will not be able to escape its heat and fire, and will be compelled to turn to God, and love God in return. For whithersoever he shall turn, he will ever be met by the immense benefits, the infinite goodness, the marvellous love of God; and, at the same time, the compulsion will grow strong with him to return love for this love, and it will so urge and impel him, that he will not be able to resist it, and he will feel himself gently compelled to follow.*

ᕷ

148. "How fair thou art, O Love, very essence of God!" (St Gertrude).*

ᕷ

RUAH   *Breathe in*   (*Puraka*)   See **62–65**

VISSHUDHA   *Hold breath*   (*Kumbhaka*)

149.   As I gently retain my breath, I concentrate on the throat-*chakra* VISSHUDHA. The Sanskrit word means literally "with purity." This *chakra* is located at the base of the throat. As my attention moves up through the throat, as through a tunnel into the region of the head, I can ask God to cleanse my thoughts, my prayer and my life. The great collect for purity at the beginning of the Anglican Eucharist is appropriate here, with its bringing together of mind and heart: "cleanse the *thoughts* of our *hearts* by the inspiration of your Holy Spirit."

ॐ

150.   On purity, Teilhard de Chardin says:

Purity does not lie in separation from, but in a deeper penetration into the universe. It is to be found in the love of that unique, boundless Essence which penetrates the inmost depths of all things and there, from within those depths, deeper than the mortal zone where individuals and multitudes struggle, works upon them and moulds them.*

ॐ

151.   I think also of my speaking, of my voice, recalling that this potent activity of my life must be purified and sanctified and that the tongue which confesses Jesus as Lord and sings the praise of God must not curse and vilify my brothers and sisters, as St James teaches (3:2–12). I may like to pause here and speak aloud some act of worship or sing a hymn, if I am so led. At all times, throughout this prayer-programme, I should be ready to vary or abandon it, if I feel the Holy Spirit may be leading me (see **9**).

ॐ

152. On the use of the voice in prayer, St Thomas Aquinas says:

> the voice is employed in individual prayer in order to pay a debt, for man ought to serve God with all that he has received from him, not only with the mind, but also with the body.

> Vocal prayer is offered, not in order to tell God something he does not know but that the minds of the person praying and even of others might be lifted up to him.*

We can use Psalm 51:15, either in its original singular form or in the plural, as in the opening of Morning and Evening Prayer in the Book of Common Prayer:

> "O Lord, open thou our lips; and our mouth shall show forth thy praise."

༝

ABBA   *Breathe out*   (*Rechaka*)   See **70–78**

RUAH   *Breathe in*   (*Puraka*)   See **62–65**

153.   As I gently hold my breath, and quietly hold in my mind the thought of purity, I fix my attention on the purity of light and darkness – the sheer blackness of the dark, and the radiant clearness of the light. They are opposites and yet they complement each other, like *yin* and *yang* (see **115–122**).

༡

154.   God is light but dwells in darkness. "God is light and *in him* there is no darkness at all" (1 John 1:5). But the light of the Godhead is surrounded by darkness, as Moses discovered on Mount Sinai. He was the founding father of mystical prayer and forerunner of all who are led to penetrate "the cloud of unknowing."

> And the people stood afar off, while Moses drew near to the thick darkness (*or* dark cloud) where God was (Exod. 20:21).

> The Lord has set the sun in the heavens,
> but has said that he would dwell in thick darkness
> (1 Kings 8:12).

St Gregory of Nyssa, the great fourth-century Greek master, wrote a "Life of Moses" and explained that Moses' experience was a sort of picure of what happens when we come to know God. At first, it is an experience of light: we come to understand things about God and the truth, we see all kinds of things clearly. But as we go on, deeper into the actual, first-hand experience of God, we leave behind what we have seen and understood, and find ourselves in a sort of fog; darkness falls; and if and when we come really close to the heart of God, we come to "see" in a different way – not like seeing objects clearly in daylight, but more like a definite experience of a real presence which is felt but not understood; a deep knowing of God, as of a dear friend who is at the same time immeasurably greater and more mysterious than we can comprehend.*

～

155. Because this is all very difficult to put into words in a straightforward way, the mystics resort to strange poetic expressions, as they try to convey to us something of their experience of the Godhead, e.g. "the radiant darkness" (Denys the Areopagite)*, "luminous darkness and rich nothing" (Walter Hilton)*; "the divine darkness, which is dark from its surpassing brightness . . . as the shining of the sun on his course is darkness to weak eyes" (John Tauler).*

～

156. St John of the Cross has taught us about the "dark night of the soul" and he has helped countless people on their spiritual journey. But we must be very careful about using, and over-using, that fascinating expression. Some people jump to the conclusion that they are experiencing the "dark night of the soul," which sounds dramatic and rather grand. But the dark night cannot simply be identified with severe depression or loss of faith or the effects of physical or psychological suffering. We should get good advice, and always remember that St John of the Cross teaches that what is important is not some spiritual state of mind but *faith* – simply "walking by faith," as the Bible says. This is beautifully put by the prophet Isaiah:

Which of you fears the Lord and obeys his servant's
commands?
The man who walks in dark places with no light,

Yet trusts in the name of the Lord and leans on his
God (Isa. 50:10).

Such a person, says the Chandogya Upanishad, will
reach "the other side of darkness"*

ᡐ

light

darkness

157.   As I gently breath out, saying LIGHT, I worship the eternal Godhead "who alone has immortality and dwells in unapproachable light, whom no man has ever seen or can see" (1 Tim. 6:16). The NEB (margin) translation of John 1:9 calls it the "light absolute".

ᠵᡄ

158.   The eternal unknowable light illumines all humankind (John 1:4). And this light came into the world (1:9) in the Word-made-flesh (1:14) and so became light in and of the world (8:12 and 12:46).

ᠵᡄ

159.   Some scientific facts and models concerning light may be of service to our meditation. Hermann Bondi says:

> Light does not age, there is no passage of time for light. This view helps to make the unique and universal character of light somewhat clearer. It cannot change once it has been produced, owing to the fact that it does not age, and therefore it must remain the same.*

Light is invisible (we see because objects emit or reflect light); it travels in straight lines; its velocity is the greatest possible speed in nature and is absolutely constant – relative to all observers, it is the same.

ᠵᡄ

160. Jesus Christ the Light of the World brought light to the eyes of the blind man (John 9); and I identify myself with him, as with blind Bartimaeus, Mary Magdalene and the thief on the cross (see **83** and **84**).

> I look to you for light
> Jesus, light of the world and of humankind.
> What do I want, O God?
> to fall into the abyss of your light
> to be lost in your light

RUAH *Breathe in* (*Puraka*) See **62–65**

AJNA *Hold breath* (*Kumbhaka*)

161. As I gently retain my breath, saying AJNA (Sanskrit "place of command"), I concentrate on the *chakra* between the eyes.

162. For the yogis, *ajna* is the chief locus of concentration: "This is the seat of the mind" (Sivananda);* it is especially associated with OM (see **165–168**); and with the command of the guru – for Christians, Jesus, above all (see **85**).

ᢞ

163. I concentrate on my mind, as the thinking activity of the self, and on my brain as the "command-centre", the control-tower of the central nervous system and the whole amazing complex of signals and responses within my body.

ᢞ

164. I recollect and offer to God my powers of deliberating, deciding and directing; the rational and responsible, conscious and volitional activity of the self; together with the autonomous nervous system which exercises its own control, awesomely, over so many functions of the body. These powers are a cause for deep thanksgiving and wonder and the giving of glory to God.

> It was you who created my inmost self,
> and put me together in my mother's womb;
> for all these mysteries I thank you:
> for the wonder of myself, for the wonder of your
> works (Ps. 139:13–14 JB).

ᢞ

ABBA *Breathe out* (*Rechaka*) See **70–78**

RUAH *Breathe in* (*Puraka*) See **62–65**

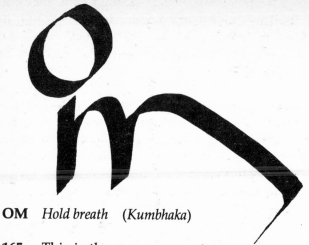

OM   *Hold breath*   (*Kumbhaka*)

165.   This is the supreme *mantra* (see **18**) for Hindus. It is a sacred sound, made up of three components: A – U – M. The A is as in "among" and the U is like the vowel-sound in "book". So the A and the U combine to make the diphthong *O*.* If you were saying OM aloud, the M, bringing the lips together, makes a deep humming at the end, which can be prolonged.

This mantra is uttered with great care and reverence by Hindus, and if we use it we should do so in the same spirit. I have heard it chanted in unison in the Sivananda *ashram* at Rishikesh, in the foothills of the Himalayas, where I stayed in 1980, and it was a memorable experience.

ॐ

166.   Dom Henri le Saux, a French Benedictine monk who adopted the Indian name Abhishiktananda, argues, in chapter 10 of his excellent book *Prayer*, that the OM can be used by Christians and says:

More than any particular name of the Divinity it conveys the ineffability and the depths of the divine

Mystery. It bears no distinct meaning . . . It does not even recall any mythological or semi-historic event. It is a kind of inarticulate exclamation uttered when man is confronted with the Presence in himself and around himself.*

Abhishiktananda warns us against careless use of the OM, since it "is too rich and too exalted for anyone to be capable of using it unless he has at least begun to taste the inner experience to which it refers. Otherwise it remains an empty sound, having no spiritual echo in the man who utters it."* But, in the same chapter, he refers to the privilege all Christians have of uttering "the sacred invocation, *Abba*, Father"; and the re-nowned Hindu swami Vivekananda has some liberal and liberating things to say on the subject: "around this word OM are centred all the different religious ideas in India," and religious believers of all kinds "and even atheists took up this Om. Om has become the one symbol for the religious aspiration of the vast majority of human beings . . . As such, it should be accepted by everyone."*

You could say that OM is the name of God which is not a name. It is a mysterious and mystical sound which suggests the infinite and eternal Godhead, God in the absolute sense, which lies behind any name or idea we could have of divine being. It does not in any way deny or diminish the Holy Name of Jesus, most precious to all Christians, or the mystic mantra which he taught us: "Abba, Father." However, if you feel uneasy about using OM, as I said above (36) just use another prayer-word. You could substitute, say, TRINITY (33).

We might think here of the "Prayer for Peace" which originated around 1981 and has been translated into more than forty languages. It is used not only by religious believers but by humanists and agnostics and generally those who believe in the power of positive thought.

Lead me from death to life
　　　from falsehood to truth
Lead me from despair to hope
　　　from fear to trust
Lead me from hate to love
　　　from war to peace
Let peace fill our heart, our world, our universe
PEACE　PEACE　PEACE.

This prayer, which has Indian antecedents, is also said with "OM – Shanti (peace) – Shanti – Shanti" at the end.

An heroic Polish priest, Stephan Kovalski, immured himself some years ago in an appalling slum in Howrah, the twin city to Calcutta. I have only been through Howrah on a bus, which means that I did not see the worst of it; but having been to some of the *bustees* of Calcutta itself, I can form some idea of what conditions were like for him. Stephan was led to use the OM, as Dominique Lapierre describes:

> A mystic invocation which for thousands of years had assisted Hindus to enter into contact with God, this *Om* diffused an ineffable inner peace. Stephan Kovalski had heard it for the first time in the villages in the south and the vibrations of this simple syllable had seemed to him to be charged with such power, such profundity of prayer, that he had adopted it to open his own invocations to the Lord. Pronouncing the *Om* required no conscious effort. "The *Om* came all by itself and prolonged itself, vibrating like a prayer in the heart," he would say.*

We should be cautious about simply imitating the spirituality of a holy man such as Stephan Kovalski; and we should be mindful of Abhishiktananda's warning; but, on balance, it seems to me that we can be free and open to the use of the OM.

167. OM represents the ultimate mystery of the Godhead, the "God beyond God" of the mystics, the "light absolute" (see **157**). Patanjali, in the Yoga Sutras, says: "His (God's) manifesting word is Om."* Swami Prabhavananda and Christopher Isherwood, in their commentary on this aphorism, claim that "OM is almost certainly the most ancient word for God that has come down to us through the ages."* Abhishiktananda quotes the Mandukya Upanishad:

> OM! This syllable is all this:
> What was, what is, what will be –
> everything is just OM!
> And whatever may transcend the three times,
> that too is just OM!*

He refers also to "the silent fourth part of OM, where every conceivable sound is left behind."*

168. Sivananda says that the three components of OM (see **165**) are associated with the colours red, white and black respectively. These colours appear in the Bible, in the books of Zecheriah (1:8, 6:2, 6:3 and 6:6) and Revelation (6:2, 6:4, 6:5). Christians who observe liturgical colours will recall those associated with the Holy Spirit (red) and Christ (white); while black might be referred to God the Father on the basis of "the thick darkness where God was" (see **154–5**) and the darkness of the Cross where Christ became lost in God when he lost himself and everything (Matt. 27:45–6; Mark 15:33–4).

St John of the Cross has some beautiful colour-imagery in the *Dark Night of the Soul*, where he speaks of "the livery" which the soul wears: "of three chief colours – white, green and purple – denoting the three theological virtues, faith, hope and charity."*

169. This Hebrew word is the sacred name *par excellence* in the Old Testament. It could be regarded as a kind of counter-balance to OM, since it is represented as divinely-revealed (Exod. 3:14–15) and, being in the *imperfect* form of the *verb* "to be", i.e. not a noun, suggests the activity of God within creation, history and humanity, rather than pure being.

ᛢ

170.   The imperfect (the only other form of verbs in Hebrew is the perfect) has the sense of unfinished action – past, present or future – or of potential: may, can, might, could, would, etc. A valid alternative translation to the usual I AM at Exodus 3:14 (put in the margin of CB and NEB) is: I WILL BE WHAT I WILL BE.

ᛢ

171.   The following quotations illustrate the profound implications for theology and prayer of such a translation:

> It has been said often in recent years that the expression used in Exodus 3:14 (*'Ehyeh asher 'ehyeh*) is correctly translated not as "I am who I am", which can be interpreted within our categories in the sense of a vigorous but static assertion of God's transcendence, but rather as "I will be who I will be." A new kind of transcendence is emphasized: God reveals himself as a force in our future and not as an ahistorical being (Gustavo Gutiérrez).*

> Certainly God is there said to be our future, but *our* future in so far as this future belongs to *itself*, is grounded in itself, and is not simply the correlative of our wishes and strivings: "I will be who I will be,"

runs the central phrase of the passage mentioned. It defines the deity of God as free, self-belonging dynamism of our future and not primarily as "Being above us," in the sense of a beyond that is to be experienced outside history (J.B. Metz).*

♈

172.   As I utter the prayer-word YAHWEH (or the poetic abbreviation JAH which appears in many song-like passages in the Old Testament, especially the HALLELUJAH [Praise the Lord] of the Psalms), I worship the God whom we encounter in history, in the events of life; who is active, dynamic, relational; who calls us into *the future*, to co-operate, as responsible beings created in his image, in the divine work; as Teilhard says of his experience:

> It was a *God of the Ahead* who had suddenly appeared athwart the *traditional God of the Above*, so that henceforth we can no longer *worship fully* unless we superimpose those two images so that they form *one*.*

♈

RUAH   *Breathe in*   (*Puraka*)   See **62–65**

173. As I gently retain my breath and say SAHAS-RARA, I concentrate on this *chakra* located at the top of the head. The Sanskrit word means "one thousand," the thousand-petaled lotus, "a number which is indicative of infinitude" (Sivananda).* The yogis envisage Kundalini reaching the apex of the self and being united with the god Siva (see **104–106**, especially **106**):

> It is here that the final union of Siva and Sakti . . . is realized, and here the *kundalini* ends its journey after traversing the six *chakras* (Mircea Eliade).*

ๆ

174. G. G. Coulton (in *Studies in Medieval Thought*) speaks of the concept in St Augustine, St Thomas Aquinas and the fourteenth-century Dominican mystics, of the apex of the mind as the point of contact with God, indeed God immanent: "a spark of divinity, *scintilla* in Aquinas, *Seelenfunklein* in Eckhart."* And the seventeenth-century Benedictine Augustine Baker speaks of:

> A drawing or draining up of the soul, or of somewhat of it . . . towards and into the head; where it seemed to him that the soul (has) a special residence and abiding place.*

This would seem to be in contrast with the Eastern Orthodox imagery of the *heart* as the "spiritual centre" of the self. However, it may be that a dynamic rather than static view of the self could reconcile these two images, along the lines of a "movement" up and beyond, and a returning down to the centre; as in

Moses' prayer of the ark during the Israelites' journey in the wilderness:

> And whenever the ark set out, Moses said, "Arise, O Lord, and let thy enemies be scattered; and let them that hate thee flee before thee." And when it rested, he said, "Return, O Lord, to the ten thousand thousands of Israel" (Num. 10:35–6).

~

175. SAHASRARA can be seen as the symbol of *the ultimate* in human aspiration, development and fulfilment; and the point of departure, going beyond the self into God: "the *sahasrara* no longer belongs to the plane of the body . . . it already designates the plane of transcendence" (Eliade).*

~

176. The "ascent" of the self to God should not be seen as a "natural" human enterprise, since we depend upon the grace of God; and we link this movement of the self through and beyond itself to the Glorious Mystery of the Ascension of the Lord; who goes before us as the "Pioneer" (Acts 3:15 and 5:31; Heb. 2:10 and 12:2) and draws us up after him into the very heart and life of the Godhead.

~

ABBA   *Breathe out*   (*Rechaka*)   See **70–78**

RUAH   *Breathe in*   (*Puraka*)   See **62–65**

177. As I gently retain the breath, I offer the prayer-word YOU. The Holy Spirit leads us on in prayer and leads us beyond the self. We must go beyond the self. Having reached the ultimate, the fullest development of the self, the most complete realization we can conceive – there is nothing now but *You O God*.

It is not necessary that we actually experience this spiritual condition. We may well be plodding modestly along the foothills of the Himalayas, rather than climbing the breathless summits. But whatever state we are in or can conceive, however exalted above the lowly state of our minds and lives – the grace of the Lord, the real presence of God, the Love which formed and indwells us are far beyond all that. What God is actually doing in us is far beyond all that.

To say YOU is only what we say whenever we recite the Lord's Prayer. What is happening here is that the process of moving imaginatively and aspirationally from the anus to the apex of the self, and then "launching out into the deep" (Luke 5:4) and coming "face to face" with God, can bring home to me what prayer actually is – any prayer, any time. I address the Lord, the God, the Father, the beginning and end of my life and all life.

Now we see the gracious work of Christ and his Spirit: leading me up, beyond, through the self, to God. Christ is indeed the Door, the Way; he leads me into the very heart of the Godhead. As he ascended into heaven (meaning that he went beyond all that is created, into the eternal and infinite glory of the Godhead) so he now kindly leads us along the same way; already in prayer he brings us face to face with God and tells us to address him as YOU, Thou.

178.   The Jewish mystical and philosophical writer Martin Buber, in his classic *I and Thou* (1923), has taught us much about the essentially relational nature of our knowledge of God. This is a special characteristic of the revelation of Jesus, as he recognizes, when he speaks of:

> the saying of *I* by Jesus! For it is the *I* of unconditional relation in which the man calls his *Thou* Father in such a way that he himself is simply Son, and nothing else but Son.*

And when Buber speaks of the child's "instinct to make everything into *Thou*, to give relation to the universe"* we may be reminded of the special title given to Jesus in the primitive Church in Jerusalem: *pais*, usually translated "servant" but could be "child" (CB margin) as recorded in four verses of Acts (3:13, 26; 4:27, 30), all of them referring to Jesus as God's "child" and in the last two, significantly, as "thy holy servant (child) Jesus," in a prayer to God. One can get a clear impression, from the sayings and attitude of Jesus in the Gospels, of one who was "a child in the universe" or "the child of the universe"; and we can meditate on the relational depth and radical reorientation implicit in the sayings about the mysteries of God being revealed to "babes" (Matt. 11:25) and our need to "become like children" (Matt. 18:3) in order to "receive" (Mark 10:15) or "enter" (Matt. 18:3) the kingdom of heaven.

Of Jesus, Buber's words are supremely apt, and they can be an objective for us: when he speaks of an attitude to God within the world, God's creation:

> to eliminate or leave behind nothing at all, to include the whole world in the *Thou*, to give the world its due and its truth, to include nothing beside God but everything in Him – this is full and complete relation.*

᠅

179. In uttering the prayer-word YOU I am turning away from the use of prayer as magic, an attempt to manipulate – and *addressing* myself personally to God, which is the essence of prayer (see **7**):

> Magic desires to obtain its effects without entering into relation, and practises its tricks in the void (Buber).*

> for we miss Him, Him who is, if we say "I believe that He is" – "He" is also a metaphor, but "Thou" is not. And yet in accordance with our nature we are continually making the eternal *Thou* into *It*, into some thing – making God into a thing (Buber).*

180. And so "all God's names are hallowed, for in them He is not merely spoken about, but also spoken to" (Buber).*

For "God is the Being that is most directly, most nearly, and lastingly, over against us, that may properly only be addressed, not expressed" (Buber).*

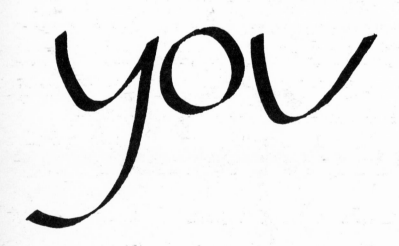

181.   As I breathe out gently I say GOD. This is a word which, for some, has become heavy with finality and foreboding, a foreclosing and even oppressive word. On the other hand, it has become over-used – "God this, God that, and God the other thing" – and even debased by zealous believers – Ian Paisley announced on the day of his election to Parliament in 1970: "This day it is known in North Antrim that there is a God in heaven!" – so that it has become seriously de-valued. But it is still serviceable, probably unavoidable and capable of beautiful resonance, especially if we recall Buber's teaching about the relational character of the knowledge of God (see **179–180**), the "content" of the name (see **185**), and see it as, in Gerard Hughes' quotation, "a beckoning word",* and as Ernest Wood says:

> a word of discovery, not a word of definition . . . a word with which to give *direction* to the mind, a word which is like a boat, such as Columbus used when he set out to discover something he did not know.*

And from another tradition (although Tao cannot be equated with God, yet there are deep affinities):

> "Tao is a name that indicates without defining."*

182. Christ has revolutionized our understanding of God, as John Macquarrie says:

> If Christ is indeed the manifestation of God in the finite, then his way through the world from the stable to the cross revolutionizes the understanding of God, and invests him with a humility, passibility and involvement with the creation which were not obvious (though they may to some extent have been latent) in the Old Testament. The trouble is that Christians have been slow to Christianize their understanding of God and seem to have a habit of lapsing back into the pre-Christian monarchical conception of God.*

And the life Christ now lives "he liveth unto God" (Rom. 6:10) and this is our end, to live "unto God", in Christ to lose our life and find it in God (Mark 8:35).

ᡐ

183. There is no need to comment further on the revelation of God as the Blessed Trinity since the whole of this book and its method of prayer exemplifies that doctrine. But we can usefully reflect here on another model of God which appears in so many different religious traditions, ancient and modern, that it must correspond to the truth of authentic experience: what has been called the "dipolarity" of the one God.

In Hinduism, Brahman is spoken of as *nirguna*, without attributes, and *saguna*, with attributes.* Tao has two aspects, conceived of as "having no name" and as "having a name."* The Jewish Kabbalah makes a distinction between God as he is in himself and in relation to creation,* while Buber says: "Of course, God is the 'wholly Other'; but He is also the wholly Same, the wholly Present."*

In the Christian tradition, Vladimir Lossky, writing about Pseudo-Dionysius (c. 500 A.D.) says that his "distinction between the unknowable essence and its natural processions or energies . . . will serve as the dogmatic foundation for the doctrine of the vision of God in later theology, especially in the fourteenth century."*

In modern times, John Macquarrie writes of A. N. Whitehead's concept of God's "primordial nature" and "consequent nature", and his "dialectical recognition of the dipolar nature of God – that he is both beyond time and in time, transcendent of the world and immanent in it, active and yet the recipient of action and even enduring suffering."* And Jim Garrison writes of Charles Hartshorne's dipolar theory of the Godhead: "God's 'abstract essence' and God's 'consequent states'";* and of Paul Tillich's theology, distinguishing between "the infinite source of all holiness" and "finite holiness" – "that which is unconditioned, inexpressible, transcendent" and "knowable, conditioned by history, experienceable by individuals."*

પ

184. From our point of view, there is God in the absolute sense and (also unknown to us) in the complex of relations with the entire universe; and in the relative sense, in relation to us and other creatures. We must hold together both aspects of the one Godhead; otherwise, God becomes either a remote cosmic force, which would effectively dissolve the truth of divine names altogether; or a local tribal deity of planet Earth and humankind, with no real connection with cosmic forces and energies. We can, in our thought and prayer, move, with "the glorious liberty of the children of God"

(Rom. 8:21) from the experience of intimacy to the apprehension of immensity and infinitude.

> In the morning, as God rises over our horizon
> the dawn-light is Love
> In the evening, as God goes down over our horizon
> the sunset-light is Love
> But what he is in himself, beyond our horizon
> who can say?

ℳ

185. We must have a real appreciation of the "content" of the holy name, the "attributes" of God, such as love and truth, beauty and goodness; and also be ready to be led beyond to the absolute Godhead, by the Spirit who "searches everything, even the depths of God" (I Cor. 2:10). It is the nature of Love (see **145–148**) not to enclose and confine but to enlarge and expand our lives and our thought, to create space for us (see **181**); as the psalmist says:

> You have set my feet: in a broad place
> > in a large room (Authorized
> > > Version)
> > where I may walk at liberty
> > > (Alternative Service Book).
> > > > (Ps. 31:8).

As Kierkegaard beautifully says of the omnipotence of God:

> Omnipotence alone can take itself back while giving, and this relationship is nothing else but the independence of the recipient. God's omnipotence is therefore his goodness. For goodness means to give absolutely, yet in such a way that by gradually taking oneself back one makes the recipient independent.

From finite power comes only dependence, and omnipotence alone can make something independent, can create something out of nothing which endures of itself, because omnipotence is always taking itself back.*

RUAH   *Breathe in*   (*Puraka*)   See **62–65**

186.   God is light but the light is "unapproachable" ("inaccessible" JB; 1 Tim. 6:16). God is light but dwells in darkness: "And the people stood afar off, while Moses drew near to the thick darkness where God was" (Exod. 20:21). "Then Solomon said, 'The Lord has set the sun in the heavens, but has said that he would dwell in thick darkness'" (1 Kings 8:12).

♈

187.   God, the absolute Godhead, in contrast with God relative to us, revealed to us, is "Wholly Other". Into this mystery of mysteries Christ leads us. God is Wholly Other – but the "other" is also, for me, the rest of Creation and especially my fellow human beings. Throughout the progression of prayer-words, I can at any point associate myself in spirit with my sisters and brothers; here, in this word which is a rehearsal for death and a sort of dying, being lost and falling – I think of those who will die with me, at the very moment of death. Who will they be? People of all ages, in all countries and societies. All together, we shall be swept up and over the crest of earthly life and descend into the Other; not to speak of the company of the Virgin Mary, the Saints and the holy Angels, especially my Guardian.

J. B. Metz writes approvingly of the Marxist Roger Garaudy's understanding of death:

> the essential removal from this death-situation of its private character, the essential reference of this experience of death to other human beings. Similarly, the Christian attitude to death must not be narrowed down to an individual aloofness from the world. It also looks towards the world, the world of our brethren.*

♈

94

188. This is the desert, the abyss, spoken of by the mystics . . . a falling desert-space, the other side of all that we know. Consider these images from two fourteenth-century mystics: "a dark Silence, a wild desert . . . the abysmal Sea . . . the wild darkness of the Godhead" (Ruysbroeck).* "God is a pure Being and a Waste of calm seclusion . . . the Wilderness of the calm and living Godhead . . . the Divine Darkness . . . the Abyss of the Divine Darkness" (Tauler).*

⟡

189. "If God were some thing, this or that, He would not be all in all, and above all, as He is . . . Therefore God is, and yet is neither this nor that which the creature, as creature, can perceive, name, conceive or express" (*Theologica Germanica*).* "There is no knowing what God is. Something we do know, namely, what God is not" (Eckhart).*

⟡

190. And the Buddha's words about Nirvana: "That abode, O brethren! has neither coming nor going, neither birth nor death. Without origin and without annihilation and beyond thought is that. The destruction of all sorrow is that. That abode, O brethren! is unborn, uncreated, unmanifested and unconditioned . . ."*

⟡

You are God and we are everything else

You are God and have no need of anything else

191. The last four phases of this exercise have no suggested prayer-words. The idea is that this can be an imageless end-prayer of silent communion with God. The method of this book, or any other method, is only a means to an end, which is God, our end and our beginning.

ᢗᢙ

192. Before the blank pages which follow, here are some thoughts as background material for this end-phase. They include images but such as point the way to imageless prayer, if the Lord grants you that. The accent is on *waiting on the Lord*, the heart of true prayer.

ᢗᢙ

193. "Prayer consists of attention. It is the orientation of all the attention of which the soul is capable towards God" (Simone Weil).*

ᢗᢙ

194. "My silence has waited long for You, and even now, in the depths of my soul, no word has ever been uttered, a wholly silent place exists, kept for the Amen of Life Eternal" (Pierre Charles).*

ᢗᢙ

195. "I would rather be a doorkeeper in the house of my God than dwell in the tents of wickedness" (Ps. 84:10).

ᢗᢙ

196. "I am the door (*thura*)" (John 10:7).

And a man lame from birth was being carried, whom they laid daily at that gate (*thura*) of the temple which is called Beautiful. . . . (Acts 3:2).

I am carried along by others, like that lame man (and see **84**) – by the prayers and loving support of the Virgin Mary, the holy Angels, and saints and friends on earth and in heaven.

Immense
overwhelming
overflowing
lifting me up
carrying me along:
the prayer of the Communion of Saints

ᡃᠣ

197. "What though a man have all the world yet must he look upon himself as poor and all the time be reaching out his hand before the door of our Lord God, asking for the grace of God. . . ." (Eckhart).*

ᡃᠣ

198. "Behold, I stand at the door (*thura*) and knock; if anyone hears my voice and opens the door, I will come in to him and eat with him, and he with me" (Rev. 3:20).

ᡃᠣ

199. "Now Moses used to take the tent and pitch it outside the camp, far off from the camp; and he called it the tent of meeting. And every one who sought the Lord would go out to the tent of meeting, which was outside the camp" (Exod. 33:7).

ᡃᠣ

200. 1 Cor. 16:22: "Our Lord, come!"

MARANATHA!

Breathe out   (Rechaka)

Breathe in   (Puraka)

Hold breath (*Kumbhaka*)

Breathe out (*Rechaka*)

References

(See note re. books on Yoga on p. 6)

Numbers refer to paragraphs in the text

11. *The Cloud of Unknowing* (14th c.) ed. C. Wolters. Harmondsworth, Middx: Penguin, 1978, cc 37 and 38. US: *Cloud of Unknowing*, Ed. by James Walsh (Classics of Western Spirituality), Mahwah, N.J.: Paulist Press, 1981.

13. Irénée Hausherr *The Name of Jesus*. Kalamazoo: Cistercian Publications, 1978, pp. 178, 220, 283, 286.

14. Cassian *Conferences* (ca. 400 A.D.). London: Thomas Richardson, n/d, Conference IX. US: *Cassian's Conferences* – Conference IX (Classics of Western Spirituality), Mahwah, N.J.: Paulist Press, 1985. *Rule of St Benedict* (6th c.). London: S.P.C.K., 1931, c. XX. US: Doubleday Image, 1975.

15. *The Pilgrim continues his Way* (19th c.) tr. R. M. French. London: S. P. C. K., 1973, p. 68. US: tr. Helen Bacovcin, Doubleday Image, 1978.

16. Benedict Zimmerman, OCD, Prefatory essay to St John of the Cross *The Ascent of Mount Carmel*. London: Thomas Baker, 1906, p. 5.

18. Ross, quoted *The Asian Journal of Thomas Merton*. London: Sheldon Press, 1974, p. 386. US: *Asian Journal*, Thomas Merton, New Directions, 1975. Raimundo Panikkar, quoted Vandana *Gurus, Ashrams and Christians*. London: Darton, Longman and Todd, 1978, p. 43.

21. Eckhart (14th c.) *Meister Eckhart*. London: Fontana, 1963, p. 151.

25. Tissa Balasuriya *Planetary Theology*. London: SCM Press, 1984, p. 273.

26. M. Eliade *Yoga*. Princeton, New Jersey: Princeton University Press, 1969, p. 4.

    Swami Sivananda *Kundalini Yoga*. Shivanandanagar (India): The Divine Life Society, 1980, p. xxxiii.

    Patanjali *Yoga Aphorisms* (300 B.C./200 A.D.) I.2. Eng. trans. (Swami Prabhavananda and Christopher Isherwood) *How to know God*. New York: Mentor, 1969, p.11.

    H. E. W. Slade, SSJE, Privately published tr. Patanjali *Yoga Aphorisms* I.2.

29. A. Louth *The Origins of the Christian Mystical Tradition*. Oxford: Clarendon Press, 1981, p. 165.

35. Bede Griffiths *Return to the Centre*. London: Fount, 1978, p. 76. US: *Return to the Center*, Templegate, 1976.

38. Swami Vivekananda *Raja-Yoga*. Calcutta: Advaita Ashrama, 1978, p. 149.

Swami Sivananda (26) p. 87.

Swami Sivananda *The Science of Pranayama*. Shivanandanagar (India): The Divine Life Society, 1978, p. 4.

A. Avalon *The Serpent Power*. New York: Dover Books, 1974, p. 76.

39. Swami Sivananda (38) p. 7.

41. Swami Sivananda (38) p. 52.

42. *The Way of a Pilgrim* (19th c.). tr. R. M. French. London: S. P. C. K., 1986, p. 10. US: Image, Helen Bacovcin, Doubleday, 1978.

43. Alan W. Watts *The Way of Zen*. Harmondsworth, Middx: Penguin, 1962, p. 217. US: Random House, 1989.

44. Barbara Brosnan *Yoga for Handicapped People*. London: Souvenir Press, 1982, p. 46.

46. M. Eliade (26) p. 410.

A. Daniélou *Yoga*. New York: University Books, 1955, p. 123.

47. Hugh of St Victor (12th c.) *Selected Spiritual Writings*. London: Faber, 1962, p. 176.

48. St Ignatius of Loyola (16th c.) *The Spiritual Exercises*. tr. W. H. Longridge, SSJE, London: Robert Scott, p. 53 (First Exercise) and p. 55. US: *Spiritual Exercises of St Ignatius of Loyola*, tr. Elizabeth N. Tetlow: College Theology Society, 1987.

49. Mahammad Abdul Aleem Siddiqui *Elementary Teachings of Islam*. Medina: Islamic Cultural Centre, 1954, p. 33.

53. Swami Sivananda (26) pp. 127–8.
Martin Smith, SSJE, *The Word is Very Near You*. London: Darton, Longman and Todd, 1990, pp. 86 and 214.

57. St Ignatius (48) p. 71 (Fourth Addition).

Patanjali *Yoga Sutras*. II.46.

Richard Rolle (14th c.) *The Fire of Love*. Harmondsworth, Middx: Penguin, 1972, p. 89.

Richard Llewelyn *With Pity not with Blame*. London: Darton, Longman and Todd, 1982, p. 107.

58. *Bhagavat Gita* (2nd c. B.C.+). 6.13.

59. St Ignatius (48) p. 164.

62. Gesenius *Hebrew and English Lexicon*.

M. Eliade (26) p. 385.

65. Bede Griffiths (35) p. 129.

The Doctrine Commission of the Church of England *We Believe in God*. London: Church House Pub., 1987, p. 120.

67. John of Ruysbroeck (14th c.) *The Adornment of the Spiritual Marriage*. London: Dent, 1916, p. 56.

68. Walter Hilton (14th c.) *The Scale of Perfection*. London: Burns & Oates, 1953, p. 79.

69. *The Exercises of St Gertrude* (12th c.). London: Burns & Oates, 1863, p. 128. US: *Spiritual Exercises*, Kalamazoo: Cistercian Publications, 1989.

Augustine Baker (17th c.) *Holy Wisdom*. London: Burns Oates & Washbourne, 1948, p. 618.

William Blake (18th c.) *Jerusalem 4*.

The Dhammapada (3rd c. B.C.) ET Juan Mascaro. Harmondsworth, Middx: Penguin, 1973, p. 9 and pp. 77–8.

70. Arndt-Gingrich *A Greek-English Lexicon of the NT*. Chicago: C.U.P., 1957.

71. J. Jeremias *The Prayers of Jesus*. London: SCM Press, 1967, p. 97 and p. 63.

72. Bishop Diadochus (5th c.), quoted J-M. Déchanet *Christian Yoga*. London: Burns & Oates, 1960, p. 193.

76. St Anselm (11th c.).

Julian of Norwich (14th c.) *Revelations of Divine Love*. Harmondsworth, Middx: Penguin, 1966, ch. 59. US: Doubleday, 1977.

77. Bede Griffiths (35) p. 27.

Bhagavat Gita (58) 9.17.

Julian of Norwich (76) ch. 59.

85. *Advaya taraka Upanishad*, quoted by A. Daniélou (46) p. 113.

88. Nyanaponika Thera *The Heart of Buddhist Meditation*. London: Rider, 1983, p. 10.

89. Bhikku Khantipalo, quoted T. Merton (18) p. 297.

J-P. de Caussade (18th c.) *Self-Abandonment to Divine Providence*. Glasgow: Fontana. US: *Abandonemnt to Divine Providence*, Tan Books Pubs, 1987.

M. Buber *I and Thou*. Edinburgh: T & T. CLark, 1937, p. 78. US: Scribner, 1979.

Ursula Fleming *Meister Eckhart*. London: Fount, 1988, p. 147.

91. A. D. Lindsay *Descartes*. London: Dent, p. 250.

Abhishiktananda *Saccidananda*. Delhi: I. S. P. C. K., 1974, p. 172.

93. J. Brabazon *Albert Schweitzer*. New York: 1975, p. 244.

94. D. H. Lawrence *The Complete Poems*. Harmondsworth, Middx: Penguin, 1977, p. 673.

95. J. Macquarrie *Paths in Spirituality*. London: SCM Press, 1972, p. 71.

97. M. K. Gandhi, quoted R. Payne *The Life and Death of Mahatma Gandhi*. p. 424.

Eckhart (14th c.) *Fragments 240*.

104. M. Eliade (26) p. 245.

J-M. Déchanet *Yoga and God*. London: Search Press, 1974, p. 96.

105. J. Garrison *The Darkness of God*. London: SCM Press, 1982, p. 127.

107. Julian of Norwich (76) ch. 60.

109. *Encyclopaedia Judaica*. Jerusalem, 1976. "SHEKHINAH".

Ibid.

Oxford Dictionary of the Christian Church. Oxford: O. U. P, 1974. "Shekinah".

116. *The Writings of Chuang Tzu* (4th c. B.C.) in *The Texts of Taoism*, tr. J. Legge. New York: Dover Books, 1962, pp. 291–2, 298–9, 332–3, 349.

118. As (116): pp. 333 and 349.

Sanmohana Tantra, quoted A. Daniélou (46) p. 126.

119. M. Milner *The Hands of the Living God*. London: Hogarth Press & I.P-A, 1969, p. 362.

124. M. Milner (119) p. 253.

130. Pope John Paul II *Redemptoris Mater*. London: C.T.S., 1987, III.47.

William Herebert (14th c.)

Pope Paul VI *Marialis Cultus*. London: C.T.S., 1974.

134. P. Berryman *The Religious Roots of Rebellion*. Maryknoll, N. Y.: Orbis, 1984, p. 278.

Frei Betto *Fidel and Religion*. New York: Simon & Schuster, 1987, p. 76.

136. M. Eliade (26) p. 242.

E. Wood *Yoga*. Hardmondsworth, Middx: Penguin, 1962, p. 169.

A. Avalon (38) p. 47.

137. A. Avalon (38) p. 53.

140. William Law (18th c.) quoted *From the Fathers to the Churches*, ed. Brother Kenneth. London: Collins, 1983, p. 422.

141. St John of Karthapos (7th c.) in *The Philokalia*, Vol. I. London: Faber & Faber, 1983, p. 319.

Chandogya Upanishad, quoted in *How to know God* (26) p. 49.

142. Theophan the Recluse (19th c.) in *The Philokalia* (141) pp. 183 and 184.

Svetasvatara Upanishad, quoted M. Eliade (26) p. 121.

Bhagavat Gita VIII.12.

143. Julian or Norwich (76) ch. 25.

Teilhard de Chardin *The Heart of Matter*. London: Collins, 1978, p. 141.

144. Cardinal Newman *Meditations and Devotions*. London: Longmans, 1953, p. 326.

J. Garrison (105) p. 133.

145. Richard Rolle (57) ch. 14.

147. John Tauler (14th c.) *Meditations on the Life and Passion of our Lord Jesus Christ*. London: Burns Oates & Washbourne, 1925, pp. 304–6.

148. St Gertrude (69) p. 99.

150. Teilhard de Chardin (143) p. 71.

152. St Thomas Aquinas (13th c.) *Summa Theologiae*. Oxford: Blackfriars, 1964, 2a 2ae Q83 Art. 12.

154. St Gregory of Nyssa (4th c.) *The Life of Moses*. New York: Paulist Press, 1978, p. 95.

155. Denys (or Dionysius) the Areopagite (fl. ca. 500) *Mystic Theology*, ch. 1, quoted E. Underhill *John of Ruysbroeck* (67) p. 255.

Walter Hilton (68) ch. 40.

John Tauler (14th c.) *The Inner Way*. London: Methuen, 1909, pp. 323–4.

156. *Chandogya Upanishad* in *Hindu Scriptures*. London: Dent, 1938, p. 184.

159. H. Bondi *Einstein and Common Sense.* Heinemann, 1965, p. 108

162. Swami Sivananda (26) p. 55.

165. Abhishiktananda *Prayer.* London: S. P. C. K., 1975, p. 59.

166. Abhishiktananda (165) p. 59.

   Abhishiktananda (165) p. 61.

   Swami Vivekananda (38) p. 143.

   Dominique Lapierre *The City of Joy.* London: Arrow Books, 1986, p. 68.

167. Swami Vivekananda (38) p. 141.

   How to Know God (26) p. 40.

   Abhishiktananda (165) p. 80.

   Abhishiktananda (91) p. 174.

168. St John of the Cross (16th c.) *Dark Night of the Soul.* London: Burns & Oates, 1976, p. 170 and pp. 170–5. US: *The Dark Night of the Soul* (from the Collected works of St. John of the Cross, ed. Kavanaugh, Rodriguez), Institute of Carmelite Studies, 1979.

171. G. Gutiérrez *A Theology of Liberation.* Maryknoll, N. Y.: Orbis; London: SCM Press, 1974, p. 164.

   J. B. Metz in R. Garaudy *From Anathema to Dialogue.* London: Collins, 1967, p. 111.

172. Teilhard de Chardin (143) p. 53.

173. Swami Sivananda (26) p. xxxix.

   M. Eliade (26) p. 243.

174. G. G. Coulton *Studies in Medieval Thought.* London: Thomas Nelson, 1940, p. 164.

   The Confessions of Father Baker (17th c.) London: Burns Oates & Washbourne, 1922, p. 107.

175. M. Eliade (26) p. 243.

178. M. Buber (89) p. 66.

   M. Buber (89) p. 27.

   M. Buber (89) p. 79.

179. M. Buber (89) p. 83.

   M. Buber (89) p. 112.

180. M. Buber (89) p. 75.

   M. Buber (89) p. 80.

181. Gerard Hughes *God of Surprises*. London: Darton Longman & Todd, 1986, p. 31.

E. Wood (136) p. 30.

T. Merton *The Way of Chuang Tzu*. New York: New Directions, 1969, p. 152.

182. J. Macquarrie *In Search of Deity*. London: SCM Press, 1984, p. 228.

183. Bede Griffiths (35) p. 122.

Tao Te Ching of Lao Tzu (6th c. B.C.) in *The Texts of Taoism* (116) p. 47.

Encyclopaedia Judaica (109) "KABBALAH".

M. Buber (89) p. 79.

V. Lossky *The Vision of God*. Leighton Buzzard: Faith Press, 1963, p. 104.

J. Macquarrie (182) pp. 148 and 150.

J. Garrison (105) p. 37.

J. Garrison (105) p. 140.

185. T. Haecker *Soren Kierkegaard*. London: OUP, 1937, p. 19.

187. J. B. Metz (171) p. 121.

188. John of Ruysbroeck (67) p. 98.

John Tauler (155) p. 324.

189. *Theologia Germanica* (14th c.) London: Stuart Watkins, 1966, p. 84.

Ursula Fleming (89) p. 114.

190. *Sermons and Sayings of the Buddha* (6th c. B.C.). Sudhakar Dikshit. Bombay: Chetana, 1977, p. 81.

193. Simone Weil *Waiting on God*. London: Fount, 1977, p. 66. US: Harper and Row, 1977.

194. P. Charles *Prayer for All Times*. London: Sands, 1929, p. 131.

197. Ursula Fleming (89) p. 158.

Indexes

Numbers in the right-hand column refer to paragraphs in the text.

1. Bible References

2. Subjects, Themes, Biblical and Holy Names
Prayer-words are in capitals

3. Authors, Books, Individuals

Summary of Prayer Words, for easy reference, together with

NB. The exercise is begun by breathing out, coupled with

Then:

RUAH	Breathe in
AWAKE	Hold breath
ABBA	Breathe out
RUAH	Breathe in
JESUS	Hold breath
RABBONI	Breathe out
RUAH	Breathe in
SATIPATTHANA	Hold breath
ABBA	Breathe out
RUAH	Breathe in
COGITO	Hold breath
TRUTH	Breathe out
RUAH	Breathe in
MULADHARA	Hold breath
ABBA	Breathe out
RUAH	Breathe in
KUNDALINI	Hold breath
SHEKINAH	Breathe out
RUAH	Breathe in
SVADISHTHANA	Hold breath
ABBA	Breathe out
RUAH	Breathe in
YANG	Hold breath
YIN	Breathe out
RUAH	Breathe in
MANIPURA	Hold breath
ABBA	Breathe out
RUAH	Breathe in
KOILIA	Hold breath
LIFE	Breathe out

breathing marks.

a prayer to, or for, the Holy Spirit.

RUAH	Breathe in
ANAHATA	Hold breath
ABBA	Breathe out
RUAH	Breathe in
KARDIA	Hold breath
LOVE	Breathe out
RUAH	Breathe in
VISSHUDA	Hold breath
ABBA	Breathe out
RUAH	Breathe in
DARKNESS	Hold breath
LIGHT	Breathe out
RUAH	Breathe in
AJNA	Hold breath
ABBA	Breathe out
RUAH	Breathe in
OM	Hold breath
YAHWEH	Breathe out
RUAH	Breathe in
SAHASRARA	Hold breath
ABBA	Breathe out
RUAH	Breathe in
YOU	Hold breath
GOD	Breathe out
RUAH	Breathe in
OTHER	Hold breath
. . .	Breathe out
. . .	Breathe in
. . .	Hold breath
. . .	Breathe out